Folger Documents of Tudor and Stuart Civilization

THE HISTORY OF ITALY

FOLGER DOCUMENTS
OF TUDOR AND STUART CIVILIZATION

THIS volume is one of a series of publications of Tudor and Stuart documents that the Folger Library proposes to bring out. These documents will consist of hitherto unprinted manuscripts as well as reprints of rare books in the Folger Library. An effort will be made to choose significant items that will throw light on the social and intellectual background of the period from 1485 to 1715. In response to almost unanimous requests of interested historians, the spelling, punctuation, and capitalization will be modernized in printed texts. In some cases, where the original printing is clear and easily read, texts may be photographically reproduced. The Folger Library is prepared to supply microfilm of original texts to scholars who require a facsimile.

THE HISTORY OF ITALY

(1549)

BY WILLIAM THOMAS

EDITED BY

George B. Parks

PUBLISHED FOR

The Folger Shakespeare Library

CORNELL UNIVERSITY PRESS

Ithaca, New York

PREFACE

THIS abridgment includes all of Thomas' own observations of and information about the Italy of his time. It omits the lengthy summaries of ancient and medieval history which he compiled from the chronicles and which have long been superseded. Thomas' knowledge of contemporary Italian history is also inadequate, but it is important as giving an English view of the Italy that he was introducing to English readers. Our edition, therefore, in retaining 162 of the 445 pages of the original, contains the essential parts of Thomas' book.

In accordance with the practice of this series, the spelling of English and Italian words, including the names of persons and places, has generally been modernized. Thomas' sprinkling of Latin and Italian words throughout his text has generally been respected, except that an occasional Latin form, such as Bononia and Placentia, has been replaced for the sake of clarity by the Italian form, here Bologna and Piacenza, and the family which he calls the Veranei becomes the Varani.

The text used is that of the Folger copy. Its editing owes much to the care and skill of Miss Ellen C. Eyler of the Folger staff.

G. B. P.

Queens College, New York
December 11, 1962

v

CONTENTS

Contents

INTRODUCTION

THIS is the first English book on Italy. It was written at the moment when a great enthusiasm suddenly arose in England for Italian culture, and the book strengthened that enthusiasm. The same moment, paradoxically enough, saw the definitive separation of England from the Church of Rome, but the repulsion seems not to have reduced the attraction. Perhaps the cultural appeal of Italy was an essential compensation for the loss of the religious tie.

The book was written by William Thomas (ca. 1507–1554), a Welshman in the English civil service (to use a modern term).[1] Thomas had enjoyed a modest success, endured some misfortunes—which however led to the writing of this book—and in the end came to a violent death. Fortune's wheel, to which men of his time ascribed the inexplicable rise and fall of men, especially men in public life, revolved more than once in his short history.

Thomas was probably educated at Oxford. He became clerk of the peace in several Welsh counties, and he received some grants of monastic property at the dissolution of the monastic orders in England. Then the wheel brought him down. In 1545,

[1] See for documentation E. R. Adair, "William Thomas: A Forgotten Clerk of the Privy Council," in *Tudor Studies* (London, 1924).

when he was probably nearing forty years of age, he suddenly became a fugitive from justice, fleeing to Venice with money belonging to his patron, Sir Anthony Browne, a prominent courtier. The Privy Council at home ordered the English diplomatic agent in Venice to have Thomas arrested for embezzlement. Venice complied, and the fugitive was required to turn over his letters of exchange (or money orders) to his patron's account. He was then released, and the agent, Edmund Harvel, reported Thomas' profuse penitence for his crime, which he ascribed to a passion for gambling. He was presently given an official pardon.

Thomas did not, however, return home at once but remained some three years in Italy. We do not know how he lived during this time, but we suppose that he was allowed to receive money from home. We can follow his movements to some extent by observing the references in his books to his stay in Florence and Bologna in the winter of 1546–1547, in Rome at Christmas of 1547, in Padua in 1547–1548, and in Naples, Genoa, Mantua, Ferrara, and Urbino at other times. He made a serious study of Italian language and literature and must have begun to write there the books which would transmit his knowledge to England.

Sir Anthony Browne died in May, 1548, and Thomas went home in that spring or summer.[2] Fortune's wheel carried him swiftly up again. He was made Clerk of the Privy Council in 1550 and became an intimate of the young King Edward VI, to whom he became a kind of tutor in political thinking. But the King died in mid-1553, and the accession of Queen Mary, which brought about the execution of Thomas' new patron, the Duke

[2] Thomas Hoby wrote in his diary that Thomas passed through Strasbourg, where Hoby was living, in January, 1547–1548, on his way home. But Thomas dated the preface to his *Italian Grammar* from Padua, February 3, 1548, and we can guess that Hoby, who wrote his diary later, had the wrong month. Hoby left Strasbourg on July 4, 1548, and Thomas must have arrived before that time. Hoby's diary is printed in Camden Society *Miscellany*, 3rd ser., X (London, 1902); the reference to Thomas is on page 4.

Introduction

of Northumberland, led to his downfall. He took part in Wyatt's rebellion, at the start of the next year, against the Spanish marriage, and he was hanged at Tyburn in February, 1554.

He had written his two books, however, which have made his fame. He published, within a year of his return from Italy, *The History of Italy* (1549; reprinted 1561). In the next year he published the *Principal Rules of the Italian Grammar* (1550; reprinted 1562 and 1567). Both were pioneer works. The *History* was, as has been said, the first English book on Italy. The *Rules* was the first Italian grammar for Englishmen and it was supplemented by a lengthy Italian-English dictionary of some 9,000 Italian words for readers of Dante, Petrarch, and Boccaccio. Most of the work on these books must have been done in Italy, since they required a very substantial amount of reading in both Italian chronicles and Italian imaginative literature, together with books on the Italian language. Thomas' three years in Italy were years of busy study and led to more significant results than most travelers can show.

British travelers had gone to Italy from the time when Claudius added Britain to the Roman Empire; their travel there became regular and a matter of course after St. Augustine of Canterbury re-established the Roman Church in England. Kings, soldiers, and diplomats, churchmen of all ranks, merchants, students, and pilgrims made the seven-week journey on horseback from London to Rome, and some left records of their journeys. Some travelers were professional writers—Alcuin, John of Salisbury, Peter of Blois, Chaucer—but only one wrote a work of any size on Italy. This was Friar John Capgrave, historian, whose *Solace of Pilgrims* (ca. 1450) gave a guidebook account (which he left sadly incomplete) of the sights of Rome as he observed them there in Holy Year. Chaucer, it is true, acquired a knowledge of Italian literature and found in it a new inspiration for English writing. Yet if Thomas in 1545 had wished to read up on Italy, he could not have found a book that was not more concerned with Italy's ancient or medieval past than with his own day. He may well have written his books to inform himself.

If Thomas was the first Briton to study seriously the Italy of his time, he was also one of the pioneers in England of the study of the Italian language. For a whole century after Chaucer it is difficult to discover any English literary interest in either the Italian language or literature in Italian. When Dante was translated for English readers, he was translated into Latin (1416); Boccaccio's works were translated either from his original Latin or from the Italian via the French. The prevalence of Latin writing by Italian writers was a main cause of this alienation, and though numerous writings of the Italian humanists were imported into England and some were published there in Latin or in English, we do not find any translations direct from the Italian published in England until Thomas Wyatt's *Certain Psalms* (1549), an abridged paraphrase of the *Penitential Psalms* of Aretino. Translations had been done before that time, but none were published.

This is not to say that Englishmen did not learn Italian, for students and diplomats and others resident in Italy for any length of time would need to do so to supplement the international language, Latin. The humanists who went to Italy in the fifteenth century to study Greek must have learned some Italian; for one, Thomas Linacre spent twelve years there as a student. But the only Englishman we know to have put his Italian knowledge to any literary use was William Lily, who translated for Thomas More (who knew no Italian) an Italian book on a dice game, the *Libro delle sorti* (1474), which he may indeed have published. Among churchmen, Cardinal Bainbridge was the first English cardinal to live in or even to visit Rome for more than a century. He had taken a degree in law at Bologna in 1492, and in 1509 he returned as ambassador to Rome, where he died in 1514. Being active in the business of the Church, even commanding a papal army, he must have spoken and written the

Introduction

Italian that was the unofficial language of the Curia. His protégé and successor as ambassador, Richard Pace, spent sixteen years in Italy as student and diplomat, and one official letter in Italian is extant in his handwriting; but his literary interest lay in translating Plutarch into Latin and in writing Latin treatises on learning. Cardinal Pole, whose elevation occurred in 1536, as a student at Padua and Venice had learned to be fluent in speaking and writing Italian, but as an attainted exile until 1553 he played no role as intermediary between Italian secular culture and England.

Thomas Wyatt was the first Englishman since Chaucer to make serious literary use of Italian by translating it into English, particularly by acclimatizing the sonnet form; his interest in Italian presumably began during his three-month mission to Italy in 1527, his only visit there. The Earl of Surrey, his junior, who never saw Italy, introduced English blank verse on the Italian model; he may have learned Italian at the French court, or indeed at the English court, where in the 1530's the language attracted special attention for political as well as literary reasons. Politically, the succession of diplomatic missions to Rome concerned with the annulment of the royal marriage may have induced Archbishop Cranmer to learn Italian. Certainly Bishop Bonner was so influenced. Thomas Cromwell, the King's minister after Wolsey, had learned the language in earlier sojourns in Italy and was a patron of persons interested in it. Cromwell employed a recent law student at the University of Padua, Richard Moryson, to write propaganda (1536–1540) against the Catholic rebels in England, and Moryson drew upon Machiavelli's recently published works for historical illustrations—not, it should be said, for any sinister doctrine of the kind that would later be called Machiavellian. The Latin writings of two Italian antipapal writers, Marsiglio of Padua and Lorenzo Valla, were published in English at just this time (1534, 1535); the former was sponsored by Cromwell, and we may conclude that Italian antipapal content joined with Italian literary eminence to create a cult of Italian at the English court.[3]

The most surprising evidence of this vogue is the interest shown in Italian by a sixty-year-old courtier, Henry Parker, Lord Morley, who had never gone to Italy. Being in the habit of presenting New Year's gifts to the King or the Princess Mary or others consisting of manuscript translations from Latin of small books or essays on devotion or morality, he learned enough Italian to make three from that language. Two had occasional value: the *Commentaries of the Turk,* a brief history of three centuries of Turkish conquest written by the contemporary Italian historian Giovio (or Jovius), was a present to the King (1536?) to remind him of that ever-present danger to the West; another warning work was a story from Masuccio's *Novellino* (no. 49) of the attempted betrayal of an Emperor by a Pope. Morley's third translation rendered an eminent piece of literature, Petrarch's *Triumphs,* which he turned into rough and unpoetic verse by 1546, though he did not publish it until after 1553.

How and why Morley learned Italian we cannot tell, except as we have inferred that it was becoming both topical and fashionable. The extent of the fashion is marked by the education of royalty. Henry VIII and his daughter Mary did not know Italian. Elizabeth was studying it, however, at the age of eleven, when, at the end of 1543, she wrote a letter in Italian to her stepmother. By 1550, Ascham reported, she could speak Italian and French as fluently as she spoke English and Latin. Her later penchant for speaking foreign languages is well known; and indeed her translation of a passage from Petrarch's *Triumphs* is far better than Morley's.

Cromwell died in 1540, Wyatt in 1542, Surrey in 1546, and still no translation direct from the Italian had been published in England except for Chaucer's works. But translating went on.

[3] *PMLA,* LXXVII (December, 1962), 529–535, for the Italian cult.

Introduction

The most surprising activity is that of the young Edward
Courtenay, son of the executed Marquis of Exeter. Although he
had been a prisoner in the Tower of London since 1539, when he
was thirteen, his education there somehow included Italian, and
in 1548 he translated a classic of Italian Protestantism, the
Beneficio di Gesu Cristo crocifisso (1542); how the book got to
England and to him in prison we have no way of knowing. It
might have been brought to him by someone like Thomas. Or
it may have been brought in by the first of the Italian refugee
divines whom Cranmer invited to England to strengthen Protestant doctrine there. It may be added that Courtenay was by no
means a devout youth, and that he was released by Queen Mary,
who could not have known about the book.

At any rate, Italian was clearly fashionable if it reached royalty at one extreme and prisoners in the Tower of London at the
other. It is ironical that this fashion developed at the very time
when England was cut off from most of Italy. The last English
mission to Rome was sent in 1534, and the last diplomatic agent
of England at the Curia died in 1536 and was not replaced.
Reginald Pole, being required to give an opinion on the King's
withdrawal from Rome, wrote in 1536 a belligerent reproof,
which won him the cardinalate but caused the execution of his
brother and mother and his own attainder. An Englishman who
ventured to go to Rome thereafter incurred the suspicion of
having "gone to Pole," and risked attainder.

The traveler to Venice was perhaps under less suspicion, if
only because an English agent was stationed there who could
and did keep track of travelers. Even so, as England moved to
doctrinal reform after Henry's death at the beginning of 1547,
suspicion naturally continued to attach to travelers who might
show or develop Catholic sympathies. In 1550 the English agent
was required to find out if two English students who had obtained degrees at Padua had sworn allegiance therefor to the
Pope. Danger also threatened from the other side, for the Inquisi-

tion was established in Rome in 1542 and in Venice in 1547. The government of Venice protected foreigners, as Thomas' book said, but Rome was soon arresting Englishmen: for example, Thomas Wilson in 1558, Thomas Sackville in 1564, and so on at times until the reign of Charles I. Englishmen could go to Italy to practice their Italian, but outside of Venice they needed to walk warily.

Despite this danger, and perhaps because the death of Henry removed a greater peril, within a year after his death upper-class youth were flocking to Italy for travel and study. It is true that this habit was not new, since students had been going to Italian universities for four centuries; as far as we can tell, however, these had been serious students bound principally for degrees in law, not the gentlemen whom Thomas in his book rejoiced to see there. The new fashion took the dilettante to Italy. Our first substantial evidence, in the absence of adequate university records, is furnished by Thomas Hoby, younger brother of an ambassador. In 1547, being seventeen, he was sent from Cambridge for a year of study at Strasbourg with Bucer and other learned Protestants. At eighteen he went on to Padua, spending a year there and a year traveling about Italy. He was not, of course, the first to go abroad to study both men and cities, as a favorite quotation from Homer then prescribed—that is, to learn to know a language and a country. But he was the first Englishman to leave a diary accounting for his movements, and this diary records the new fashion.

Hoby wrote down the names of Englishmen whom he met in Italy on errands similar to his own: fourteen at Padua in 1548–1549, thirteen others at Siena, Rome, and Naples in the next year, and in 1554–1555, during the Marian exile, sixteen of student age at Padua.[4] The numbers are altogether surprising and without precedent. An English "nation," an association of English law students, had been in existence at the University

[4] Camden Society *Miscellany*, 3rd ser., X, 8, 19, 24, 116–117.

of Padua since 1222, but in the earlier sixteenth century only an occasional Englishman could be found at Padua to be an official of the nation, as, for example, Richard Moryson in 1534. From 1550 there is no lack.[5]

We may guess that the death of King Henry made travel abroad easier. We may guess that the example of Thomas Smith, who came back to Cambridge in 1542 with a degree from Padua to become Regius Professor of Law, may have encouraged Cambridge students to follow him. Hoby was one, and William Barker, John Handford, George Harding, Henry Killegrew, and perhaps John Christopherson, were some of the others. Hoby went on to Florence, Siena, Rome, Naples, Calabria, finding other Englishmen of his class in the cities and accompanying them or running into them again on his way. The effect in 1548–1550 is that of a company of young Englishmen "doing" Italy.

When Thomas passed through on his way home to England in the spring of 1548, Hoby was still in Strasbourg, with his journey ahead of him. The *History* was written by then, and Thomas had also written for an English friend in Venice the first Italian grammar for English use. These books came at exactly the right moment to reach the new English audience at home and abroad. The grammar (published in 1550) would teach the rudiments of Italian, and since it included a vocabulary for readers of Dante, Petrarch, and Boccaccio, it opened the way to Italian literature as well. This literature, Thomas wrote in the dedication, came close to equaling Greek and Latin: "You shall almost find no part of the sciences, no part of any worthy history, no part of eloquence, nor any part of fine poesy, that ye have not in the Italian tongue."

The *History of Italy* in its turn opened the way to Italy itself —to "the Italian nation, which seemeth to flourish in civility

[5] Joannes Aloysius Andrich, *De natione Anglica et Scota juristarum Universitatis Patavinae* (Padua, 1892).

most of all other at this day." This meant not merely polite manners: it meant that the Italians were most civilized—as we should say, politically and socially sophisticated. The book with this theme effectively marks the beginning of the English admiration for Italy that was to be the *grande passion* of the Elizabethans and that was to persist in cultural matters at least for a full century, until the time when John Evelyn and John Milton made their journeys to Italy the summit of their education.

History included, then as now, a description of the country discussed and a record of its past, the latter being often little more than a chronology of its rulers. Much the same material went into the new world geographies, which of course added maps and a little physical geography but which retained, especially for an ancient country like Italy, a surprising amount of history, mostly ancient. Sebastian Franck's *Weltbuch* (Tübingen, 1534), for example, allowing twelve pages to Italy, gave to each of the seventeen regions only the boundaries, the names of its cities, and some anecdotal impressions of people or manners, quite as often ancient as modern. Franck writes of Campania:

Campania, a region of this often described kingdom [of Naples], now called Terra Laboris, situate between Latium and Calabria. Fruitful mountains, valleys, and fields: therefore by some called mother of fruits. In it are Capua, Nola, Naples, [which is] the noble and royal capital and seat of the king. This city is glorified with a fine harbor and splendid buildings. These peoples have ruled and held sway: Normans 136 years, Germans 76, French 78, Aragonese 60. In 1501 this kingdom came again to the French [p. lxxiii ᵛ].

Of Venice:

Venetia, a mighty region of Italy. Therein a city was built by Eneto or Veneto and the city and country called Venedig after him. Thither by necessity of war many Italians fled and thought themselves safe there, and in this country built many habitations well protected, of which we have heard elsewhere: therefore I will refrain from discussing it. Moreover the city's strength is well known to many of us. The rule of the Venetians extends so far that with their power, together with the situation of the country, they fear none in this trade center and port for Italy, Asia, Turkey, and Heathendom. It has many powerful merchants, any one of whom might buy a prince out of his country with ready money. Here are all kinds of artistic skill, able soldiers by sea or land, and their own dukedom, history, and everything as if they were a separate world. The breadth and length of their territory is extensive and seemingly endless [fols. lxxiii ᵛ–lxxiv].

This is general, but at least appreciative. The chapter on Tuscia or Tuscany is, however, merely perfunctory, with nothing on the country or the government and only slight mention of the cities but with anecdotes of witchcraft and of ancient bacchanalia. For a last section on "Italian Manners, Government, Religion, and Rule," Franck has this to say:

This land is a noble region of Europe, and among the western countries the mother and queen, rich with metal, good air [climate], fruitful ground, grain, woods, fields, meadows, cattle, game, oil, vineyards, rivers, seas, and, as it were, a warehouse of all handicraft and commercial treasure [fol. lxxiv ᵛ].[6]

These are mostly Pliny's words (*Natural History,* III, v).

Sebastian Münster's *Cosmographey oder Beschreibung aller Länder* (Basle, 1544) sensibly departs from the eleven or seventeen or more provinces of Italy to describe five principal regions: Rome, Venice, Lombardy, Genoa, and Naples (pp. xcii–cxxvii). His descriptions vary a great deal in relevancy, as if his authorities were uneven—and neither he nor Franck seems to have actually traveled in Italy; but Münster is especially concerned to bring in historical material. His Italy begins, in fact, with Janus teaching basic crafts to the original peoples. His Rome is mostly about Romulus and the founding. Venice likewise begins

[6] I thank Professor Lienhard Bergel for help with this translation.

with the founding and the first succession of dukes; but then Münster describes at length from a recent treatise [7] the powers of the Doge and follows with an account of the expansion of the Venetian empire from the year 1202. Lombardy is given an extensive history from the Lombards to the Battle of Pavia in 1525. Naples is given a historical account to 1503.

History, ancient and medieval, dominates the work, but this is not to say that Münster does not draw some shrewd geographical generalizations. He begins his section on Italy with a neat picture of the country, *ein beschlossen land,* protected by a mighty mountain range and by surrounding seas which form a moat (p. xcii). After four of the five regions he draws a picture of the fruitfulness of all Italy (p. cxiii), which he attributes to the temperate air, the many harbors, the fertile valleys and streams of the Apennines, the natural resources of mines, wine, and wool, and, finally, the superiority of the Latin tongue, which civilized the barbarian invaders. (The last item is also from Pliny.) Münster is also prone to give anecdotes from Roman history and from natural history; even his chapter "Von den sitten und brüchen der Italianer" is mostly about ancient Rome, until it surprisingly ends: "Now in our time, what Italian usage and customs are is well known. The Papacy counts for so much therein that all Christian virtue has diminished" (p. cxv). Although Münster was a Protestant, this is about his only reference to the Roman Church.

Münster's 1550 expansion to a large Latin *Cosmographia* nearly triples (to 124 pages) his account of Italy, adding excellent maps, much further history, and some contemporary observation. The edition appeared after Thomas' book, of course, but it may still be relevant to note some of his additions as running parallel to what Thomas included. Münster now has a description (pp. 145–148) of ancient Rome, hill by hill, a list-

---

[7] Gasparo Contarini, *De magistratibus et republica Venetorum* (Paris, 1543).

ing of the gates of Rome, and a fine two-page panorama of contemporary Rome, which, however, pictures the older St. Peter's as still intact. A description of a 1544 discovery in Rome of a coffin containing imperial treasure is almost the only contemporary report for the city. The rest of the account of Rome once more repeats the story of Romulus.

The material on Venice gives a description of the contemporary pageantry of the Ascension Day wedding of Venice with the sea and adds a fine two-page map. The passage builds up to a panegyric:

That most magnificent, beautiful, and wealthy city has become the queen of the sea and is inhabited by a very great number of people of many nations, who have flocked hither from almost the whole world in the pursuit of trade. And there all tongues are spoken, and there are the most disparate of human costumes. The taxes which the government collects on wine, salt, oil, and so on are said to amount to two million (twenty hundred thousand) ducats, in addition to the levies, taxes, and revenues which they draw from their subject cities [p. 155].

Other contemporary notes have been added. Duke Ercole of Ferrara is called the richest of Italian princes (p. 187). Florence is given this tribute:

This city abounds in all the comforts of living. It has the most excellent wines. It produces men of great ability and trained in all occupations. They flourish equally in learning and in war. They excel in merchandise; they have no equals in the art of building. They wear modest and sober clothing; in learning and in elegance of speech they easily surpass other Tuscans. They enjoy a climate which is most temperate and serene, since they are not more than two days distant from the sea [p. 195].

A striking addition is a report of Pisa, with special note of the Cathedral square with the Baptistery and the Leaning Tower (p. 195). The history of the Emperors surprisingly adds an account of the sack of Rome in 1527 by the imperial troops.

Introduction

The nature of these works parallel to Thomas' is described to illustrate the interests of the educated reader in a kind of informal geography. For Franck and Münster this kind was made up of much history, often ancient and generally chronological, some political geography, and some impressions of products and people. If we turn to what might seem to be more formal geography, the contemporary editions of Ptolemy's classic work with new maps, we discover again an unexpected combination of matter. Münster edited Ptolemy in 1540, and the Ptolemy text involving Italy gives little more than the latitude and longitude of numerous cities.[8] This mathematical geography is supplemented by an extraordinary Appendix Geographica, presumably written by Münster, which for Italy contains a set of extravagant stereotypes of human geography, doubtless to provide a human touch. The portion quoted below follows immediately after the praise of the resources of Italy which was to reappear in Münster's next work.

In complexion and stature the people of Cisalpine Gaul and the Venetian corner differ from the Italians: the complexion white, their dress and speech more careful. On the contrary, in Tuscany, Latium, Campania, the Abruzzi, the hair is black, they are shorter of stature and thin, their speech and dress plain. All [Italians] do not have the same manners or living habits or even laws, some following canon law, some imperial, some municipal. They all agree on living frugally, dressing handsomely, shaving their heads, wearing short Spanish cloaks which do not cover the thighs.

The Venetians, whose city enjoys the most wealth derived from both sea and land, dress in a loose gown, such as is worn by the Greeks, Turks, Russians, and other northern peoples. They so delight in the clothes of their ancestors that often the descendants wear the

---

[8] Liber III, "Italiae Situs," pp. 30–37, together with "Tabula VI Europae." It is interesting that while the latitudes are not far off, the longitudes make a distance of 13 degrees between Genoa and Otranto, instead of the actual 9½ degrees. Accordingly, on sixteenth-century maps the peninsula extends much more nearly west-east than northwest-southeast.

clothes of their great-grandfathers. They abound in deliberation, being slow of speech and unpleasant in delivery, using a ridiculous kind of magniloquence, lavish in words but empty of content. They pretend to forgive affronts, but, if ever they find occasion, no one takes a more cruel revenge. They universally swear horrifying oaths and blasphemies against God.

The Milanese, detesting the French, but hating the Spaniards quite as much, trust neither. Their speech is rough, their language violent, and the Piedmontese are even rougher and more annoying. In war they [the Milanese] are valiant only in a crowd.

The speech of the Genoese is ludicrous, nor can it be well written down; their costume is elegant, neither military nor the long gown. They are quite inconsistent in judgment and unreliable, apt for rebellion, inhospitable, and unmindful of benefits received. . . .

The Neapolitans spurn all good counsel, being rustic, talkative, flatterers, strenuous avengers of affronts, ever mindful of benefits. They like clouded faces, daubed and painted, in the women they love; nor do they love anyone who is not of high rank and followed by a flock of handmaidens. They affect Spanish speech, and in the Spanish manner ride, take part in tourneys, and display great dexterity of body on horseback. They dress splendidly, breathe balsam, eat more sugar than bread, and like to feed on cabbage. The Neapolitans jeer at the Calabrians, the Calabrians at the Apulians; the Romans jeer at all these, and the Tuscans at the Romans, who reciprocate; but the Italians jeer at all other men, whom they contemn and call barbarous, although they have been the prey at one time of the Spaniards, at another of the French, at another of the Germans [pp. 172–173].

Although some of this matter is obviously good observation, much is vicious stereotype, and it is a relief to return to Thomas. His aim was clearly to report firsthand impressions of place and society, together with basic history brought down to contemporary relevancy. Of the 438 pages of his text, 314 are devoted to history—or rather to chronology. Most of this history is, of course, mere compilation, since Thomas can claim no authority as a historian, and most of it is therefore omitted here. We retain in our text only the portions of the history nearest to Thomas' own time, which he may have modified from his own knowledge or which in any case give a useful background for the Tudor knowledge of Italy. The history of the Empire to Charlemagne can have only doubtful academic value, but the recent history of the conquests and defeats of Venice and Genoa, and the reports of the reigning ducal families of Milan, Ferrara, Mantua, and Urbino have immediate current value.

What, then, has Thomas to say about Italy? Certainly not, or not significantly, that it was once the seat of empire, the *caput mundi,* as he would have said if he had written one or more centuries earlier. In Rome he was, of course, moved by the melancholy contrast between the dismal ruins of the present and the great monuments of the past, but this was a traditional theme. He is not concerned with Italy as the seat of the Church either. He is, it is true, impressed by the splendor of the public processions of the Pope, but only as characteristic Italian pageantry, not as religious spectacle. Thomas is a Protestant and, as such, must find a focus other than Rome for his admiration. Nor was Thomas obviously a scholar, for he has nothing to say of that Italian learning which had drawn students from all parts of Europe to find there the intellectual treasures of antiquity. It is true that he mentions at the beginning the "excellent learned men" in whom Italy abounds; but he seems more impressed by the fact that 1,000 of the 1,500 students at the University of Padua are gentlemen.

Since he cannot be classed among the usual types of traveler, Thomas may best be viewed as approaching that Renaissance ideal of Ulysses, who in Homer's phrase "knew many men's manners, and saw many cities." [9] In other words, Thomas was

[9] Thomas Watson's version of line 3 of the *Odyssey,* as quoted by Roger Ascham in *The Schoolmaster* (1570); Arber ed. (London, 1870), p. 73.

the social observer, the first in England to write down what Italy was like as a society to live in.

His impression throughout is of wealth and cultivation. Italy is a wealthy land by reason of its trade to all the world and has wonderful food, especially fruit, which abounds in summer. It has impressive monuments and pageantry. It is more important that Italy honors trade, that its principal merchants are gentlemen, and that its workmen are unsurpassed for skill. For manners, Italian gentlemen are models of behavior: "so honorable, so courteous, so prudent, and so grave withal that it should seem each one of them to have had a princely bringing-up." They have "majesty" of presence, modesty of speech, refinement of appearance, complete lack of meddlesome curiosity; ladies and courtesans alike are lavishly attired.

Dark moral spots are observed: deadly revenge for insults (though Thomas makes no reference to the hired assassinations or the poisonings which were later to be thought the rule) and the stinginess and open lechery of the Venetians. This last trait horrified Roger Ascham, royal secretary, when he spent nine days in Venice in 1552: "I saw in that little time in one city more liberty to sin than ever I heard tell of in our noble city of London in nine years." [10] Ascham began the deprecation of Italians as immoral and irreligious.

One other dark spot for Thomas was the exploitation of the peasant by the landowner and (as Thomas may well have thought) by the inexorable local tax on every commodity brought to market. In other respects he presents society as admirably conducted, especially in the delicately balanced structure of the Venetian government, which was the admiration of Europe, and in the maintenance of public order and the repression of crime. Jonson's *Volpone* (1605) emphasized this concept of Venetian justice.

[10] *Ibid.*, p. 83.

Introduction

Thomas' enthusiasm then runs off into separate channels of discussion of the major Italian states. In dealing with them, he sheds the geographers' preoccupation with the ancient provinces and deals only with the contemporary states: Naples, to include Campania, Apulia, and other ancient provinces; Milan, Mantua, and Ferrara, to replace a diverse Lombardy; and Florence, to replace an earlier Etruria or Tuscia, for the grand duchy of Tuscany was not yet official. It will be seen that his enthusiasms in Rome were directed to the mighty ruins and to the luxurious parade of the Church; in Venice, to the wealth and power of the state and to the model complex government by an aristocracy; in Florence, to the tasteful display of the wealth of a city of merchants; in Genoa, to a greater and more impressive display of wealth; in Milan, as indeed in most of Italy, to the lavish wealth provided by nature. These admirations attest the respect of the northerner for the marvels of nature and of corresponding human achievement in the ideal climate midway between equator and pole—this had been a geographical commonplace since Pliny. Whether such respect has yet become wonder before "the palms and temples of the South," as a later romanticism phrased it, is not clear, for Thomas has not yet the language to express romantic wonder. The effect is, however, the same, that of being overcome after his fashion by the marvelous South.

The idea of a society of superior cultivation is less easy for Thomas to demonstrate, because he seems to have observed it only in Venice and Florence. It is too soon to expect an awareness of the fine arts for themselves and as the product of a refined society: like other travelers of his time, Thomas can speak of buildings only as sumptuous or magnificent, and painting, sculpture, and music go unnoticed. Aside from his incidental appreciation of literature, he is obliged to fall back on manners in his cultivated society: courtesy, tolerance, taste, education, and the habit of conversation—which might lead, as Thomas noted in Florence, to talk for the mere sake of talk. He did, in fact, try his hand elsewhere at an imaginary dialogue with Italian speakers. Perhaps while he was still in Italy, he drew up an account of a conversation at Bologna with "seven or eight" Italian gentlemen; but the conversation consisted entirely of Thomas' triumphant exoneration of Henry VIII, just deceased, of numerous charges leveled in Italy against his tyranny.[11] Of the Italians in the dialogue it can be said only that they were excessively tolerant, beyond all the requirements of politeness, of Thomas' intolerable girding at their church.

Meanwhile a book had been written, as Thomas knew, which eminently illustrated the ideal cultivation of Italian society. This was *Il cortegiano* of Baldassare Castiglione, published in 1528, a spirited discussion of the new ideal of the gentleman in the post-chivalric world. This literary masterpiece was translated into English in Italy by Thomas Hoby and published in 1561 as *The Book of the Courtier*. Several later English editions and a Latin version prepared and printed in England gave the picture of Italian society that Thomas tried to draw. The searching, vivacious, and inspired dialogue of *The Courtier* was far above Thomas' modest reach, as it was above the reach of most writers of dialogue since Plato, and its picture of the many-gifted but modest gentleman in a dazzling society still represents an admired ideal. The innumerable editions of the book in the principal languages of Europe show its value in the sixteenth century, and its popularity in England may have helped to eclipse Thomas' book.

Nonetheless, his *Italy* was the first, and for a long time the only, introduction to the country in English. An account of the

[11] The dialogue, with the title "Pelegrine," was not printed in English at the time; it was edited, not from the best manuscript, by J. A. Froude in 1861 as *The Pilgrim*. (A better title would be "The Traveler" or "The Stranger," since Thomas was in no sense a pilgrim.) A translation into Italian as *Il pellegrino inglese* was published in 1552, presumably in a Protestant country for propaganda in Italy. See Bibliography.

kingdom of Naples, translated from a German author, was published in 1575.[12] Many diaries of travel to Italy were kept, but most remained unpublished and it is not until the next century that any substantial book was written on Italy. Even then the only full account is Fynes Moryson's *Itinerary* (1617), describing his journeys in the 1590's through nine countries, including Italy, and, in parts still unpublished, his surveys of the governments of those countries. Indeed, we must wait until 1660 for a full English guidebook to Italy, and that was a translation of a Flemish author, Franciscus Schott, whose book (*Itinerarii Italiae rerumque Romanarum libri tres*) was originally published as early as 1600.

Naturally, many books in other languages, particularly Italian, were available to the traveler. The Elizabethan who stayed at home may well have preferred the sensational new Italian fiction, which poured into England in translation in the 1560's and 1570's, for it pictured an Italy that may have been polite but was distinguished by a passion for bloody revenge. It was this imagined Italy that inspired the Elizabethan dramatists who wrote *Othello, The Malcontent,* and *The White Devil.* The picture of society in such plays owed little to Thomas. His description of Italy was modest and truthful, and his book is still the first book to read for those who wish to study the long history of English attraction to Italy.

[12] Jerome Turler, *The Traveller,* from *De peregrinatione, et agro neapolitano* (Strasbourg, 1574).

THE HISTORY OF ITALY

A Book Exceeding Profitable to Be Read
Because It Entreateth of the State
of Many and Divers Commonwealths,
How They Have Been and Now Be Governed

(1549)

By William Thomas

To the right honorable and mine especial good lord, John, Earl of Warwick, Viscount Lisle, knight of the most noble Order of the Garter, Lord Great Chamberlain, and High Admiral of England [1]

THOUGH many wise and learned men have so substantially set forth the infinite commodities [2] that grow of the reading of histories that my wits cannot attain to a small part of the due commendation thereof, yet seeing my travail at this present hath been to publish unto our own nation in our mother tongue the doings of strangers [3] and specially of the Italian nation, which seemeth to flourish in civility [4] most of all other at this day, methought I could no less do for the encouraging of them that shall take this book in hand than partly rehearse [5] what profit they may gather by traveling therein. First, they shall see upon what little beginning many great states have risen, and how they that have had the power to rule, by using their authorities well and prudently, have merited immortal fame of honor and praise and, by using tyranny and ill governance, have contrariwise borne eternal slander and shame. It encourageth the virtuous men, by the examples that they read, to

---

[1] Warwick was rising to be the most powerful man in England, becoming Duke of Northumberland in 1551. His support of his daughter-in-law, Lady Jane Grey, against the Princess Mary led to his downfall and execution in 1553.

[2] Advantages.   [3] Foreigners.

[4] "Civility" may mean either good government (politically) or refinement (personally).

[5] Give an account of.

3

increase in virtue and nobility and showeth the vicious what the fruit of their abuses are and how naughty [6] doings have most commonly naughty ending. It moveth the noble prince to maintain peace and justice, and showeth the tyrant what plagues follow of war and cruelty and that though his tyranny pass unplagued in this world (which happeneth seldom) yet shall his name be hated and cursed in all ages and amongst all nations, as Nero, Heliogabalus, and such other princes be. It showeth also how mutable fortune is, and how that which hath been gotten with extreme pains, unmeasurable expenses, and unreasonable effusion of blood hath been lost in a moment, and that commonly he that hath conquered most in war at the best is yet a loser, and, finally, that of division [7]—either amongst the nobility or the commons—there ensueth utter destruction of realms and subversion of commonwealths, whereunto there is none so great a minister [8] as the alteration of ancient laws and customs.

All these things, with infinite mo, histories do so set forth to the eyes of princes (if they read them well) that their hearts shall be more inclined with peace and justice to enrich their subjects and thereby procure themselves glory than by murdering of innocents, ravishing of honest wives and maidens, burning, spoiling, and destruction of countries (which are the effects of war) to make themselves conquerors of that they cannot long enjoy. For surely more praise shall that prince deserve that leaveth his realm quiet and wealthy unto his successor than he that for the conquest of other countries impoverisheth and disturbeth his own.

And because this little work declareth both these extremities, as well what a number of beautiful cities have been edified and what great countries have been enriched by peace and concord, as also how many goodly things and wonderful regions have been destroyed by strife and war, therefore would I wish all

[6] Wicked. [7] Faction. [8] Agent.

noblemen to read it, to the end they may hereof take occasion so honorably to spend their lifetime that after their death they may shine in fame forever.

And knowing your lordship for your excellent feats of chivalry, both by sea and land, to be such a one as is able to judge whether mine opinion be good or not—like as your wonderful knowledge in civil orders [9] hath made you worthy to be no less esteemed excellent in counsel than as you have been tried a most valiant captain in the wars—I therefore could find none to whom I might so worthily dedicate my little travail as to you, most humbly beseeching your lordship to accept it at my poor hands as the gift of him that wisheth you all health and honor. At London the twentieth day of September, 1549.

Your good lordship's most humble at commandment,

WILLIAM THOMAS

[We omit the eight-page index—sigs. 1–(4)—which follows in the 1549 edition.]

[9] Government.

The Description of Italy

ITALY containeth in length from Augusta Praetoria [1] unto Otranto 1,020 miles, and in breadth from the river Varo [2] in Provence to the river Arsia [3] in Friuli (which is the broadest place) 410 miles, and in the narrow places, as from the mouth of Pescara to the mouth of Tiber, 126 miles. So that to compass it by sea from Varo to Arsia are 3,038 miles, which with the 410 miles by land maketh the whole circuit to be 3,448 miles. Thus it appeareth that it is almost an island, closed on the east side with the sea Adriaticum and on the south and west with the sea Tyrrhenum, which is a part of the great sea Mediterraneum. And from the north it hath the mightiest mountains of all Europe, called Alps, which divideth it from all other regions. The fashion [4] (as Pliny describeth it) is like unto an oaken leaf with the stalk, but it endeth in manner of the Amazons' targe.

It hath a very temperate and wholesome air, fertile fields,

[1] Aosta, in the northwest Alps at the foot of the Great St. Bernard Pass.
[2] The Var, a little west of Nice.
[3] A little east of Pola, opposite Venice. Arsia is the Latin form, the Italian being Arsa. The numbers in this sentence are from Pliny (III, v), except that the third number is given by Pliny as 136. Pliny's figure for the total circuit is 2,049 miles, which is more credible than Thomas' 3,448 or Leandro Alberti's 4,740 or even 4,900 (*Descrittione di tutta Italia*, [Bologna, 1550], fol. 5).
[4] Shape.

pleasant hills, batful [5] pastures, shadowing woods, plenty of all
kind of trees and groves, abundance of corn, vines, and olives,
good wools, fair cattle, and so many springs, fountains, lakes,
rivers, and havens that it is an open lap to receive the trade of
all countries; and, as it were to offer all men help, it seemeth
willingly to put itself into the sea.

It lieth between the sixth hour and the first of the winter,[6] in
manner halfway between the equinoctial and the pole, between
(I say) the heat of the sun and the cold of the north. For the
city of Bologna (where the great resort of scholars from all
nations is wont to be) standeth almost in the heart of Italy and
hath in his elevation 44 degrees, so that dividing the quarter
from the equinoctial to the septentrion into 90, according to the
rule of cosmography, and taking the one half thereof, which is
45, the difference is little, to prove that Italy is in the midst between the extremities of heat and cold. And seeing then that
temperature is it that most of all other comforteth, nourisheth,
and maintaineth nature, it must needs follow that this, being
one of the most indifferent [7] regions, must be very pleasant, delicate, and abundant.

This little discourse I have made to the intent the wise may
the better understand the cause of those things that to my purpose I must hereafter treat upon.

The commodities [8] of Italy

If I should go about to describe unto you particularly how
commodious the country is, as well to the traffic [9] of them that
live by merchandise as to the good lief [10] of them that love their
rest, it should be enough alone to occupy an whole volume, but

[5] Rich. This paragraph is also from Pliny.

[6] This phrase from Pliny meant only that Italy extends to south-southeast,
halfway between noon (south) and winter sunrise (south-southeast).

[7] Balanced.   [8] Here meaning "products."   [9] Trade.

[10] Liking.

because I would seem no more tedious in this than I covet to do in all the rest, I say:

First, for merchandise, Italy, as an heart or knot of these parts on our half of the world, is the principal place of recourse of all nations that occupy [11] anything of importance far from home. For like as with us in England the most merchants of the realm resort to London to utter [12] their own wares and to buy such other as make for their purposes, even so they of France, of Spain, of Germany, and of all other westerly places that covet the merchandise of Syria, Egypt, Cyprus, Candia, Constantinople, and those other easterly parts, as jewels, drugs, spices, perfumes, silks, cotton, sugar, malmseys,[13] and otherlike, resort most commonly into Italy with their wools, cloths, linen, leather, metals, and such other, to Genoa, Milan, Venice, Ancona, Messina, Naples, or to some of those places whereas traffic is used, and there, meeting with Jews, Turks, Greeks, Moors, and other easterly merchants, selling the one, they buy the other.

Then, for pleasure, he that hath mean to pay for that he taketh shall have in Italy what he can reasonably desire: fine bread, singular good wines both strong and small, flesh of all sorts both wild and tame, fowl of all kinds both of water and land, fish as well of the sea as of the fresh water, but specially such plenty of delicate fruits as would make a man leave flesh, fowl, and fish to eat them, namely in the summer. I mean the melons, pepons,[14] pomegranates, oranges, lemons, citrons, and sweet grapes, besides their figs, apples, pears, peaches, plums, and olives, with a thousand other of that sort. And it is not to be marveled at though (as the fame goeth) the Italian be a small eater of flesh. For though herebefore I have commended the temperature of Italy to be comparable with any other country, yet must you understand that in summer the sun is somewhat fervent, and in time of that heat the lightness of those sweet

[11] Engage in.   [12] Sell.   [13] Sweet wines from Greece.
[14] Pumpkins.

fresh fruits is better to be digested than the heaviness of flesh or fish, which would not there be so lightly [15] digested. As I myself have proved, that beforetime could in manner brook no fruit, and yet after I had been awhile in Italy I fell so in love withal that as long as I was there I desired no meat more because methought nothing more wholesome, specially in summer. And albeit the heat be (as I have said) somewhat fervent, yet it exceedeth not so much at the hottest as the winter cold is temperate at the coldest. For at the most the cold there endureth not three months of the twelve, and some years in manner you shall feel no winter at all.

These rehearsed commodities, with infinite other too long here to treat of, together with the loving company of the Italians (who in manner make more of strangers than of their own), do cause the infinite resort of all nations that continually is seen there. And I think verily that in one region of all the world again are not half so many strangers as in Italy, specially of gentlemen, whose resort thither is principally under pretense of study. For there are divers famous cities that be privileged with great liberties for all scholars that come, as Padua, Bologna, Pavia, Ferrara, Pisa, and others; in every one of the which are excellent learned men, waged [16] for the reading of philosophy, of the civil laws, and of all the liberal sciences, besides excellent masters of music to sing and play on all manner of instruments and the best masters of fence at all weapons that can be found. So that all kinds of virtue [17] may there be learned, and therefore are those places accordingly furnished, not of such students alone as most commonly are brought up in our universities (mean men's children set to school in hope to live upon hired learning), but for the more part of noblemen's sons and of the best gentlemen, that study more for knowledge and pleasure than for curiosity or lucre. For lightly [18] there passeth no

[15] Easily. [16] Hired. [17] Accomplishments.
[18] Here meaning "commonly."

Shrovetide without running at the tilt, tourneying, fighting at the barriers, and otherlike feats of arms, handled and furnished after the best sort; the greatest doers whereof are scholars.

This last winter, lying in Padua, with diligent search I learned that the number of scholars there was little less than fifteen hundred; whereof I dare say a thousand at the least were gentlemen.

Of the Italian customs and nature

The inheritance of lands in Italy goeth by gavelkind, that is, to wit: one brother as good part as another. So that if a *conte* (which is as much to say as an earl) have twenty sons, every one of them is called *conte,* and the youngest hath as good part in his father's lands and goods as the eldest, unless it be in the estates of princes, as of Mantua, Ferrara, Urbino, and such others, which the eldest evermore enjoyeth. And by this mean it is come to pass that in process of time, with change from wealth to poverty, there be divers earls and marquises without land or goods, retaining nevertheless the glory of that name to them and theirs forever.

But to speak of the gentlemen that have whereof worshipfully to live (which for the most part do commonly profess arms),[19] meseemeth that none other nation is like them in majesty.

First, to rehearse the conformity of speech that is amongst themselves (considering what a number of diversities they have in their tongue), it is a marvel that in manner all gentlemen do speak the courtesan.[20] For notwithstanding that between the Florentine and Venetian is great diversity in speech, as with us between a Londoner and a Yorkshireman, and likewise between the Milanese and the Roman, the Neapolitan and the Genoese, yet by the tongue you shall not lightly discern of what part of

[19] Are soldiers.
[20] Court speech. Thomas here properly translated *lingua cortegiana* as "courtesan," which had not yet been limited to the meaning "prostitute."

the country any gentleman is, because that, being children, they are brought up in the courtesan only. And generally (a few cities excepted), in manners and conditions they are no less agreeable than in their speech: so honorable, so courteous, so prudent, and so grave withal that it should seem each one of them to have had a princely bringing-up; to his superior obedient, to his equal humble, and to his inferior gentle and courteous; amiable to a stranger and desirous with courtesy to win his love.

I grant that in the expense or loan of his money for a stranger he is ware and will be at no more cost than he is sure either to save by or to have thanks for; wherein I rather can commend him than otherwise. But this is out of doubt: a stranger cannot be better entertained nor more honorably entreated than amongst the Italians.

They are very modest in their apparel, fine in trimming[21] of their houses, and exceeding neat at their table. But above all other, they are sober of speech, enemies of ill report, and so tender over their own good name (which they call their honor) that whosoever speaketh ill of one of them shall die for it, if the party slandered may know it and find time and place to do it. Whereof there is a use grown amongst them that few gentlemen go abroad unarmed. And though some in this case do discommend them, yet mine opinion doth rather allow than blame them. For the fear of such dangers maketh men so ware of their tongues that a man may go twenty years through Italy without finding reproach or villainy,[22] unless he provoke it himself.

And if one gentleman happen to defame another, many times the defamed maketh his defiance by a writ called *cartello*[23] and openly challengeth the defamer to fight in camp;[24] so that there are seen sometime worthy trials[25] between them.

[21] Furnishing.   [22] Insult.   [23] Challenge (*cartello di sfida*).
[24] Field (of duel).   [25] Contests.

And it is true that many years ago such contention hath grown amongst them that almost the whole nation hath been divided into partakings, as Guelfi and Ghibellini, imperial and French, with otherlike, which hath been occasion of much manslaughter and, consequently, of their foresaid continual use in wearing of armor.[26] But at this day those open contentions are wonderfully abated; whether it proceed of weariness or of wisdom I cannot tell.

Finally, in one thing I can singularly commend them: that they will not lightly meddle with other men's matters and that when they hear ill report they do their best to cover the slander, saying that no man liveth without fault, or with some other such reason. But like as I could reckon in the Italians' commendation many things more than are here rehearsed, even so on the other side if I were disposed to speak of vice I might happen to find a number as ill as in any other men, which are better untouched than spoken of. For whereas temperance, modesty, and other civil virtues excel in the number of the Italian nobility more than in the nobility of any other nation that I know, so undoubtedly the fleshly appetite with unnatural heat and other things in them that be vicious do pass all the terms of reason or honesty.

And yet it is not to be forgotten that these gentlemen generally profess three things: the first is arms, to maintain withal his honor; the second is love, to show himself gentle and not cruel of nature; and the third is learning, to be able to know, to understand, and to utter his opinion in matters of weight.

The principal merchants are for the most part gentlemen. For when there be of one house three or four brethren, lightly one or two of them dispose themselves to merchandise. And if they happen not to divide their father's patrimony and substance (as many times they do not), then do the merchants travail as

[26] Arms.

13

well for the wealth of their brethren as their own, for all runneth in common, be it gain or loss. Indeed, their outward profession agreeth not with the gentlemen before rehearsed. For they carry neither weapon nor armor but do what they can to live in peace, not only searching the trades of all countries with their merchandise but also occupying at home the most substantial farms [27] and possessions by their factors,[28] as hereafter more plainly it followeth. And because these merchants have nothing the less reputation of nobility for their trade of merchandise, therefore it followeth that there be such numbers of wealthy men in that country as the like is not to be found any otherwhere. For in divers cities of Italy it is no marvel to see twenty persons in a city worth 100,000 crowns [29] apiece and upwards.

As for the artificers, I have nothing to say, saving that for the most part they are the finest workmen and best inventors of all other and are so well paid for it that many of them live as well as they that have standing livings [30] and grow sometimes unto great wealth and riches, but not lightly in two or three descents unto any reputation of nobility.

The husbandmen are of all hands oppressed. For in the country there dwelleth no man of substance. All the gentlemen and other that are wealthy dwell in the walled cities and towns, leaving the villages, fields, and pastures in their tenants' hands, not to farm [31] at certain rent, as we do in England, but to the halves or to the third of all grain and fruit, as the ground is fertile or barren. And the poor tenant is bound to till, sow, and husband the ground at his own cost and charge. So that the

---

[27] Leases, or contracts to "farm out" taxes.   [28] Agents.

[29] Thomas' figure of 100,000 crowns, equaling £25,000 sterling, amounts to nearly half of the total expenditure (£56,000) of the English government in 1546. (See Frederick Charles Dietz, "Finances of Edward VI and Mary," in *Smith College Studies in History*, III [1918], 69.) We shall see that several small Italian states were wealthier than England.

[30] Established incomes.   [31] Lease.

14

landlord's part cometh clear without disbursing of a penny. And at the harvest and vintage the landlord sendeth a man of his for his part, who first taketh his choice of the grain, wine, oil, and fruit, and then leaveth the rest to the tenant as his part ariseth to. And many times, if the landlord be cruel, when he cannot sell his things at his own price, then forceth he his tenant to utter it for him and to pay for it not as he can sell it but as the landlord will. By reason whereof the poor man is brought so low that he is not able sometimes to find bread of *sorgo* [32] (a very vile [33] grain) to feed his poor children withal.

And because I have here named *sorgo*, methinketh it meet to tell that in Italy groweth many sorts of grain, as this *sorgo*, *miglio*,[34] *segale*,[35] and twenty such other—which cannot be expressed by any English names because in England there is no kind of such grain. All which serve to make coarse bread for the poor people and also for the staple of victuals in strongholds, for the bread made thereof (specially of *miglio*) will endure a number of years uncorrupted. And in like manner they have certain kinds of other grain that in general are called *legumi* [36] (as we were wont to call peasen [37] Lenten stuff), whereof they use all the year long to make their pottages.

Finally, in the villages are many fair houses made only for the owners' pastime against the heat of the summer. For then do they abandon the cities and go unto those houses for a month, two, or three, where under the fresh arbors, hedges, and boughs, amongst the delicate fruits, they triumph in as much pleasure as may be imagined. And for the most part each man hath his make,[38] with some instruments of music and such other things as serve for his recreation. And if ever the tenant

---

[32] Sorghum.   [33] Cheap.
[34] Millet.   [35] Rye.
[36] Originally meaning "pulse" (peas, beans, lentils, etc.).   [37] Peas.
[38] Mate. ("Mate" and "make" were parallel words in Old English.)

have good day,[39] then licketh he his lips of his master's leavings. As for the women:

> Some be wondrous gay,
> And some go as they may.
> Some at liberty do swim afloat,
> And some would fain, but they cannot.
> Some be merry, I wot well why,
> And some beguile the husband with finger in the eye.
> Some be married against their will,
> And therefore some abide maidens still.
> In effect they are women all,
> Ever have been and ever shall.

But, in good earnest, the gentlewomen generally for gorgeous attire, apparel, and jewels exceed, I think, all other women of our known world. I mean as well the courtesans as the married women. For in some places of Italy, specially where churchmen do reign, you shall find of that sort of women in rich apparel, in furniture of household, in service, in horse and hackney, and in all things that appertain to a delicate lady, so well furnished that to see one of them unknowingly she should seem rather of the quality of a princess than of a common woman.[40] But because I have to speak hereafter in particular, I will forbear to treat any further of them in this place.

Of the states of Italy

The greatest prince of dominion there at this present is Charles the Fifth, Emperor of Almain, who for his part hath the realm of Naples and the duchy of Milan, which realm is divided into eight regions; and to the intent the readers may the better be satisfied, I have set forth as well the ancient names of those regions as the present.

[39] Pays a visit.   [40] Prostitute.

Description of Italy

The realm of Naples

The present names	The ancient
Part of { Campagna di Roma / Maremma	Latium
Terra di Lavoro	Campania
Principato	Picentini
Basilicata	Lucania
Calabria	{ Brutii / Grecia magna
Terra d' Otranto [41]	{ Salentine / Calabria antiqua / Iapygia / Messapia
Puglia	{ Apulia Peucetia / Aetolia / Apulia Daunia
Abruzzo	{ Frentani / Peligni / Marrucini / Vestini / Precutii / Marsi
Valle Beneventana	Samnites

[41] This southeastern tip of the peninsula was eventually to be accepted as part of Apulia, to which it had in effect belonged since the Lombard invasion. Its original (Roman) separateness was still influential, however, and Alberti, for example, set up Terra d' Otranto, Terra di Bari, and Puglia Piana (or Daunia) as three separate regions.

17

As for that part of the duchy of Milan that the Emperor hath, it lieth in Lombardy, anciently called *Gallia Cisalpina,* for the most part on that side of the river Po that was called *Transpadana.*

The Bishop of Rome hath for his part the city of Rome, with these countries following:

| Part of | Campagna | Latium |
| | Maremma | |

Part of Tuscany	Etruria
The duchy of Spoleto	Umbria
Marca d'Ancona	Picenum
Romagna	Flaminia
	Emilia

The city of Bologna

The Venetians for their part have the city of Venice with those towns in and about their marsh, called *la Contrada di Venetia, la Marca Trivigiana,* and a great part of Lombardy, anciently called *Gallia Cisalpina,* on the same side of the Po that was called *Transpadana,* and part of the country of Istria.

The commonwealth of Genoa have the country about them now called *il Genovesato* and, anciently, *Liguria.*

Tuscany, anciently called *Etruria,* is divided into divers dominions; whereof a small part the Bishop of Rome hath, but the greatest is the Duke of Florence, who hath seven cities under him. And then there be two commonwealths, Siena and Lucca, whose territories are not great.

The Duke of Ferrara hath part of Romagna and part of Lombardy. The Duke of Mantua is all in Lombardy. And the Duke of Urbino is between Marca d'Ancona and Tuscany, whose people are called of Pliny *Metaurensi.* The cities of Parma and

Piacenza in Lombardy have been of late transposed from the
Church unto the state of a duchy, but now it is divided again,
as hereafter you shall perceive.

Now here is to be noted that every particular prince and
commonwealth of Italy within his own dominion accounteth
himself absolute lord and king and liveth upon the customs,
taxes, and tallages [42] that he raiseth of his subjects. For lightly
they have little or no lands at all of their own. And generally
they proceed altogether by the civil laws [43] and are so diligent
in the administration of justice, specially against murderers
and thieves, that I think no country more quiet than it—the
realm of Naples and some part of the Roman territory excepted,
where many times happeneth much robbing by the ways.

An Abridgment of the State of Italy from the Beginning until the Roman Empire Was Utterly Divided

AFTER the general flood remained no mo but Noah, his three
sons, and their wives, between whom it should seem the whole
world was divided. Shem took the east part, Ham the south,
and Japheth the west. Some write that Japheth was the same
Janus that first reigned in Italy and some that Janus was
Japheth's son. But whether so it be, this Janus was ever taken
for father of the gods and was painted with two faces, either because he was father of two nations, the Greeks and Italians, or
else because the month of January (which hath two respects,
one to the beginning and another to the end of the year) took

[42] Taxes levied upon tenants. [43] Roman law.

name of him. While this Janus reigned in Italy, Saturn, being chased out of the realm of Candia by his son Jupiter, came in a manner naked unto him, and Janus not only received him but also gave him the half of his dominion. For memory whereof either of them builded a city to his own name, that is, to wit, Janicula and Saturnia.

[There follows the history of the rulers of Italy, with Latinus, Aeneas, and the predecessors of Romulus and Remus, the kings, the consuls, the emperors, the Goths and the division of the Empire, the Lombards, and, ultimately, Charlemagne. We omit twenty-six pages here. The last paragraph of this outline (on fol. 21^v) reads:]

And thus, since Charlemagne, the Occidental empire continued under the French dominion till Gregory the Fifth, Bishop of Rome, transported the election of the Emperor unto the princes of Germany, which to this day endureth. Like as on the other side the Oriental empire continued in Constantinople in the hands of Christians till Mahomet, the second of that name, Emperor of the Turks, took the city by force, slew the Emperor Sigismond,[1] and consequently enjoyed the whole Greekish empire, as his successors do unto this day.

The Description of Rome

THINKING to find a great contentation in the sight of Rome, because that amongst all the cities of the world none hath been more famous than it, I disposed myself to go thither. But when

---

[1] The Emperor was Constantine Paleologus.

Description of Rome

I came there and beheld the wonderful majesty of buildings that the only roots thereof do yet represent, the huge temples, the infinite great palaces, the unmeasurable pillars—most part of one piece, fine marble, and well wrought—the goodly arches of triumph, the bains,[1] the conduits of water, the images[2] as well of brass as of marble, the obelisks, and a number of other-like things, not to be found again throughout an whole world, imagining withal what majesty the city might be of when all these things flourished, then did it grieve me to see the only jewel, mirror, mistress, and beauty of this world, that never had her like nor (as I think) never shall, lie so desolate and disfigured that there is no lamentable case to be heard or loathsome thing to be seen that may be compared to a small part of it. Nevertheless, when I remembered again the occasions whereof these glorious things have grown, what numbers of wars the Romans have maintained with infinite bloodshedding, destructions of whole countries, ravishments of chaste women, sack, spoil, tributes, oppression of commonwealths, and a thousand other tyrannies, without the which the Romans could never have achieved the perfection of so many wonders as mine eye did there behold, then perceived I how just the judgment of God is that hath made those antiquities to remain as a foul spoil of the Roman pride and for a witness to the world's end of their tyranny. So that I wot not whether[3] of these two is greater: either the glory of that fame that the Romans purchased with their wonderful conquests, or their present miserable state with the deformity of their antiquities.

Of the river of Tiber

The river of Tiber, which runneth through Rome, divideth Tuscany and Campagna,[4] so that Transtyberim and the Vatican, wherein standeth St. Peter's Church with the Bishop's palace

[1] Baths.   [2] Statues.   [3] Which.
[4] Thomas writes "Champaign."

and Castle St. Angelo, are in Tuscany, and the rest on the other side of the water, which is very Rome indeed, is in Campagna.

The distance between the city and the sea called *Mare Tyrrhenum* is fifteen miles. And albeit the river is great, deep, and large enough for a haven from the sea to Rome, yet most commonly the ships can come no nearer than Ostia, which is twelve miles from Rome, partly by reason of the stream that runneth very swift and partly by reason of the wonderful quantity of mud that, being brought down with the swift course of the water, lieth commonly at the mouth of the haven. So that all the merchandise, victuals, and other things that come by ship are discharged at Ostia into certain small vessels and so brought to Rome, either drawn by cord or towed up by force of oars.

The head or first spring of Tiber is in the Apennine Hills, somewhat higher than the head of the river Arno that runneth through Florence, and ere ever it come at Rome it receiveth forty-two other rivers; so that it is no marvel though it be deep, specially in Rome and to the seawards, where it appeareth that the natural breadth of it is restrained and by force of strong banks made much narrower than his ancient course hath been.

Of the bridges

Upon this river of Tiber in Rome be four bridges. The first and fairest is it that passeth from the city unto Castel S. Angelo, under the which the river coming from the north toward the south entereth into the city, and is commonly called *Ponte di Sant' Angelo* or *del Castello*. The second is Ponte Sisto, otherwise called *Ponte Rotto*, a very goodly bridge that leadeth from the street now called *Julia* unto the foot of the hill anciently called *Janiculus* in Transtyberim. The third is called *Ponte de l'Isola, Ponte di San Bartolommeo,* or *Ponte di Quattro Capi,* which passeth from the heart of the city through the island Tiberina into Transtyberim. The fourth, next to the going forth of the river out of the city at the south, is called *Ponte di Santa Maria.*

But to satisfy them that be learned, I think meet to rehearse here the names of the eight bridges, Sublicius, Palatinus, Fabricius, Cestius, Januclensis, Vaticanus, Aelius, and Milvius, and to declare where they stood.[5]

First, Sublicius, which Horatius alone defended in the wars of Porsena, was at the foot of the hill Aventine, where now is no bridge at all, and first it was made of timber, afterwards of stone by Aemilius Lepidus, for the which he was surnamed Lapideus, but finally it was made of marble by Antoninus Pius, and now decayed to the foundations, whereof parts are yet to be seen. The second, Palatinus, is now called *di Santa Maria.* The third and fourth, Fabricius, next the city side, and Cestius, on the side of Transtyberim, are the two bridges that pass through the island Tiberina. The fifth, Januclensis, is now called *Ponte Sisto.* The sixth, Vaticanus, is decayed to the foundation, part whereof is seen against the Hospital di Santo Spirito. The seventh, Aelius, is now called *del Castello.* The eighth, Milvius, is two mile northwards out at the gate called *del Popolo* in the way to Tuscany and is called at this date *Ponte Molle.*

Of the walls

The circuit of the city about by the walls, as Pliny writeth, was in his time twenty miles, and Flavius Vopiscus saith that the Emperor Aurelius 200 years before the coming of the Goths enlarged the circuit of Rome to fifty miles (whether these authors included the suburbs I cannot tell); but once there, can be seen no sign or token of any walls that should contain so much compass, nor yet of the walls that Livy mentioneth should be made of square stone. For the walls now about Rome are of brick and, in my judgment, pass not fourteen miles in compass.

---

[5] These names had become standard. This paragraph and the next are from Andrea Fulvio, *Antiquitates urbis* (1527), book III; the preceding paragraph is Thomas' own.

Nor I cannot perceive, either by mine own eye or by writing of authors or yet by report, that ever the walls were of greater circuit than they be at this present. It is evident that many parts of the same wall have been thrown to the earth by divers enemies and repaired again. For notwithstanding it be builded of brick, yet doth it show such an antique majesty (having 365 towers, agreeable with the number of days in the year) that he who seeth it must needs confess it could never be builded but in time of the Romans' glory. Perchance some will marvel how brick should so long continue, but their brick, whether it be long of good making or of the heat of the sun that drieth much better than with us, is wonderful durable. For there be many buildings in Rome of brick that have continued these thousand years and more and yet to this hour are nothing worn or decayed. Indeed, many gates of the city are of square stone, wrought after the most antique fashion, so that it is not incredible, as Livy writeth, that the walls have been of square stone, but it should not seem so because that in making of a new wall in the same place it is to be supposed the builders would have used the old square stone rather than brick.

Of the gates

Pliny writeth that in his time were thirty gates open and seven closed, but because he hath not written their names, I will not travail to try what they were. For I can find but sixteen that are used, of which four are in the Vatican that, many years after Pliny, was walled by Leo the Fourth, Bishop of Rome, for defense of his own palace and of St. Peter's Church.

First, next unto the coming down of Tiber on the north side is the gate called *Porta del Popolo,* which anciently hath had divers names, as *Flumentana* and *Flaminia* of the Way Flaminia that went out thereat.[6]

---

[6] The listing of the gates, which is substantially correct, is condensed from Fulvio, book I, with charges derived from Flavio Biondo, *Romain-staurata* (1481).

Then coming about towards the east, the next gate is called *Pinciana,* sometime *Collatina.* The third: *Salaria,* anciently called *Quirinalis* or *Agonalis.* The fourth: *Porta di Sant' Agnese,* sometime *Viminalis, Figulensis,* and *Nomentana.* The fifth: *Porta di San Lorenzo,* sometime called *Tiburtina* after some authors and after other *Esquilina,* though Andreas Fulvius affirmeth plainly Esquilina to be between this and the next gate. The sixth, *Porta Maggiore,* was sometime called *Nevia, Labicana,* and *Praenestina.* The seventh, *Porta di San Giovanni,* hath been called *Celimontana* and *Asinaria,* by reason it lieth towards the realm of Naples that breedeth many asses. The eighth, *Porta Latina,* hath not changed name, or if it be changed, the ancient name cannot be known now. The ninth, *Porta di San Sebastiano,* was sometime called *Appia* and *Capena,* and after most opinions was also called *Triumphalis.* The tenth, *Porta di San Paolo,* was sometime called *Trigemina.* All which ten gates are on the Campagna side of the river. The eleventh: *Porta Portese* or *Porta di Ripa.* The twelfth: *Porta di San Pancrazio,* sometime called *Aurelia.* The thirteenth: *Porta del Torrione.* The fourteenth: *Porta Portusa,* on the top of the hill behind St. Peter's. The fifteenth hath divers names, as *Porta di Belvedere, di San Piero, del Giardino,* or *di San Peregrino,* and is hard under the Bishop's palace. The sixteenth, *Porta del Castello,* sometime *Posterula,* lieth under Castel Sant' Angelo and serveth to go into the meadows. As for those ancient names, *Carmentalis, Pandana, Mugonia, Querquetulana, Lavernalis, Rudusculana, Rhutumena, Catularia,* and divers others, which as I suppose were old gates that lost their places as the walls were enlarged, I could never learn where they should be and therefore do believe they have been converted to the use of other buildings.[7]

These gates and walls about Rome are not strong, nor yet fortified with rampires of earth or otherwise to defend shot of artillery, and in many places are so decayed that to assault there

[7] These are the names of the gates in the earlier Servian wall, which Thomas found listed in Fulvio.

needeth not much battery. Many of the gates have been exceeding fair, but like as most notable things there be decayed, so are these rather a figure of their antiquity than anything else.

Of the seven hills

The seven hills whereon Rome standeth are but of a small height, standing arow upon the riverside.[8]

The greatest of them eastwards is called *Aventinus,* wherein was the cave of Cacus, the giant that Hercules slew, and the fountain where the gods Picus and Faunus were taken by the policy [9] of Numa, who, giving them wine instead of water, made them drunk and so took them asleep. And albeit that on this hill have been many goodly edifices, as the temples of Matuta, Diana, Minerva, Lucina, Libertas, with divers others, yet at this day there is nothing to be seen, not so much as a token of Claudius' notable conduit that Frontinus and Cassiodorus treat so much upon. For there is now none other building but the monasteries of Santa Sabina and Sant' Alessio, with a few other little churches. The rest is either covered with rubble or occupied with vines.

The next hill, first called *Tarpeius,* after *Capitolinus,* and now *Campidoglio,* was the principal place of the city, such as, for example, the Guildhall is in London. For thither came all they that happened to be received with triumph, and amongst all the buildings of the world Capitolium was counted the goodliest. For Cassiodorus saith, "It is a great wonder to behold the market place of Trajan, but to climb up into the Capitol—O there is the excellency of all human wits to be regarded!" Cicero calleth it in many places the habitation of the gods, and Vergil, the golden Capitoline. Whereof at this day remaineth no more but an old house called the Senate and the Church of Ara Coeli.

---

[8] The names of the hills come from Fulvio, book II, but rearranged and the descriptions expanded.

[9] Stratagem.

Description of Rome

They say that the Temple of Jupiter Optimus Maximus was there where the Church of San Salvator in Massimi [10] is now, and the Temple of Janus Custos where the prisons be now, called *la Cancellaria*.[11] But of their antiquity appeareth at this date not so much as the bare foundations.

Next unto Campidoglio is the hill Palatinus, on the which the emperors, kings, consuls, and other chief officers had their palaces, besides many famous temples that have been built there, whereof remaineth none other now but the old ruins and a Church of St. Nicholas,[12] not yet finished.

Here is to be noted that these three hills, Aventinus, Capitolinus, and Palatinus, were only closed with walls by Romulus, so that Rome was nothing so great in circuit at the first as it is now. But as the people multiplied, so the other hills were taken in, as he that readeth Livy shall well perceive. In effect, setting the rubble and old monstrous foundations apart, Rome (as touching these three hills) is returned desert, pasture, and vineyards, as it was before the first foundation.

Next is the hill Celius, wherein is seen unto this day a part of the ancient Roman majesty by the marvelous buildings that yet remain, not whole but so that the magnificence thereof may be comprehended, as the Amphitheatrum, now called *Coliseo,* the conduits and bains, the great palace,[13] and a number of fair churches translated from old temples.

[10] Formerly on the north slope of the Capitoline, taken down in 1567.

[11] Thomas seems to have come down from the Capitoline to the prison by the river, where the Church of S. Nicola in Carcere is; this late (Byzantine) prison included in its site the ruins of a temple of Janus among others. It is not clear whether Thomas thought this prison was the important Mamertine or Tullianum, which is in the Forum.

[12] A Church of St. Nicholas on the Palatine is mentioned by Schott, who calls it tiny (*picciola* in the Italian version), and by Lucio Mauro (*Le antichità della citta di Roma* [Venice, 1542]), who calls it a *chiesolina*.

[13] This may have been the baths of Titus or of Trajan, then visible above the Colosseum, or the ruins of the Palace of Constantine adjoining the Lateran Palace; the latter were soon to be built over by the Hospital of

Next unto this is Esquilinus, which, as Varro saith, are two hills, but they seem not so to me. In this part are Therme Dioclesiane, the Pillar of Hadrian,[14] the tower dei Conti, Trofei di Caio Mario,[15] the garden and tower of Maecenas,[16] so much renowned, with divers other things, and [it] is well inhabited.

Finally, the hills Viminalis and Quirinalis lie so together that I could not divide them. But by estimation and report they begin at the gate of St. Agnes and stretch down by Monte Cavallo unto Tiber. In which are few notable things to be seen except Monte Cavallo,[17] Therme Constantiniane,[18] Torre delle Milizie, and a few others.

Now that part of the city that is called Transtyberim is divided in two: that is, to wit, the Vatican and Janiculum.

The Vatican was walled about by Leo the Fourth, Bishop, and called *Citta Leonina* after his own name, and is well known from Janiculum because that going from the one to the other it behooveth to pass through the gate called *Septimiana,* sometimes called *Subtus Janum* or *Fontinalis;* whereby it is evident that the Vatican or Borgo San Pietro (as they now call it) was never any part of Rome until Leo's time. But Janiculum in

S. Giovanni. Thomas' map of Rome, which he might have bought in a bookstore in Venice or in Rome, was probably meager. Bufalini's large map of 1551 would have been most useful.

[14] An error for Trajan's pillar. This error is found in the map of Rome in Münster's *Cosmographia* (1550), and Thomas must have seen an earlier version of that map.

[15] Actually an ancient fountain, its ruins still extant in the present Piazza Vittorio Emanuele II. It was thought in the Middle Ages to be a monument to Caius Marius for his victory over the Cimbri and was hung with shields and other trophies.

[16] Still undisturbed, in Thomas' time, in the open country near the present railroad station.

[17] The Quirinal, so called from the statues of Castor and Pollux with horses, then in the ruins of the Baths of Constantine.

[18] Below and across from the present Quirinal Palace; they were taken down for the Palazzo Rospigliosi (1603).

Description of Rome

Transtyberim was joined unto Rome by Ancus Marcius, fourth king of the Romans, and is affirmed to be the same city that the god Janus builded and dwelled in; like as many write Saturnia, that Saturn builded, was against it on the other side of the water in the place that we call now *Campidoglio,* though some hold opinion it should be at Sutri.

Of the conduits of water

Frontinus writeth that for the space of 441 years after the edification of Rome the Romans used none other but the water of Tiber, or of such wells and springs as were found within the city. But from the time of Appius Claudius they have had so much water brought by conduits upon arches, through the mountains and some underground, that no city of all the world could be better served. And the manner was this: when they had taken a spring and had brought the water of it to the city, then was there a place made to receive it, closed about with walls like a castle, from the which pipes were laid to serve as well the common people in the open streets as also the nobility and such as were able to have water in their own houses. And so (as Strabo writeth) it seemed that rivers ran abundantly through the city, and almost every house had channels and conduits with cisterns to preserve the water. For Marcus Agrippa in one year caused 700 ponds, 105 fountains, and 130 castles to be made, besides a number of other goodly edifices for the maintenance of these fresh waters, amongst which I shall recite the principalest.

First, the water called *Appia* was conveyed upon high arches of stone out of the Lucullana territory the space of eight miles and brought in between the hill Aventine and the hill Celius; but now there remaineth nothing of them that can be seen.

Another, Aqua Marcia, sometime called *Anfeia,* lastly *Trajana,* came out of the Lake Fucinus and served principally to drink, where most part of the rest served for other uses; and this was brought by mine through the mountains and by arches above-ground twenty-three miles.

Aqua Claudia was brought thirty-five miles from two fountains, Ceruleus and Curtius, part of the way upon wonderful arches of square stone, which are yet to be seen both within and many miles without the city. Pliny saith that the conveyance of this water did cost 555,000 sestertia, which make above 60,-000 talents, and reckoning every talent at 130 pound sterling (which I think was the least), the sum amounted to seven millions and eight hundred thousand pounds of our money; which as it seemeth a sum impossible to be gathered together and more incredible to be spent in one work, so is the majesty of that building wonderful, that in manner I am abashed to write the truth thereof, for I would not have believed it myself if I had not seen it. And Frontinus writeth that these arches in some places were 109 foot high.

Then was there the old and the new Aniena, the one whereof was brought forty-two miles off and at length joineth with the water Claudia and is received upon those arches before mentioned.

Divers other waters there were, too long here to reckon; because of all these waters that were wont to come to Rome can be found no more at this day but one, called *Triviana* and anciently named *Virginia,* which cometh under the ground by the gate Pinciana and surgeth under the hill called *Monte degli Hortuli,*[19] from whence it is conveyed abroad to serve all parts of the city, because in Rome there is none other good water to drink.

Of the decay not only of these conduits but also of the other antiquities be divers opinions. Some affirm that the Goths, the Vandals, and the other barbarous nations that so often destroyed Rome were causers and doers of it. Some others ascribe the fault to time—mother and consumer of all things. Others say

[19] Between the Pincian Gate and Trinità dei Monti, then empty country.

that neither the barbarous nations nor yet time ought to be blamed for it, but rather the greedy beastliness of them that both within the city and without regarded not to spoil those noble antiquities to garnish and beautify therewith their private buildings.

Of the thermes

You shall understand that the Romans used oftentimes to bathe themselves; wherefore at the first private men made them stufes [20] or hothouses of their own. But afterwards (as a thing necessary for the commonweal), the emperors gave themselves to the making of these thermes; of which Blondus reckoneth twelve and Fulvius saith eighteen, naming them Agrippine, Neroniane, Alexandrine, Titiane, Dioclesiane, and the rest. These were not only common bains for washing but also sumptuous halls, goodly chambers, fair walking places, and every other gallant building that might serve for the commodity of them that thither resorted. The pavements were of fine marble wrought in colors, the vaults sustained on rich pillars of porphyry and finest marble of one piece, a number of hothouses in every therme, some several [21] and some common, with lodgings according and offices assigned for the service of them that would eat there, besides all other pleasures that were to be imagined, insomuch that the emperors themselves many times would come thither openly and be washed in the common houses. For it is written that the Emperor Hadrian entered on a day into one of the bains and, finding an old soldier there rubbing himself against the marble stones, asked him why he did so. The soldier answered, because he had no servant. This answer so much pleased the Emperor that straightway he not only gave this soldier a servant but also honestly wherewith to maintain him. Through the fame whereof, the next day when the Emperor came to the same bain, divers old men were gotten in before and were like-

[20] Hot baths (Latin and Italian *stufa*, stove).   [21] Privately owned.

wise rubbing themselves; who, being demanded why they did so, answered, because they had no servants. But Hadrian, perceiving their intent, called them to him and showed them how they might well enough one rub another.

Of all these goodly thermes there remaineth none other but the broken walls and the old monstrous ruins, specially of those two that were the greatest, Antoninianae [22] and Dioclesiane, whose hugeness may be reckoned as a wonder amongst the buildings of the world.

Of the naumachiae

There were certain ponds of water called *naumachiae*, made of purpose so large that small ships might meet in them. For like as the Romans were diligent in bringing up their youth in feats of chivalry, so also they exercised them in practice of the water to make them no less expert by sea than by land; for the which these naumachiae were made, specially for the triumphing days when they used to fight ship with ship and when also on the land the horsemen should be proving of their strengths. So that in one spectacle you should behold the feats of arms both by sea and land, as most commonly in Circulo Maximo it was wont to be. But at this day there scarcely appeareth any sign or token of those ponds, save that every man there can tell where some of them have been, as that before the front of Palazzo Maggiore,[23] another under Monte degli Hortuli, and one of Nero's in the Vatican. For now, through lack of water since the decay of the conduits, they are become dry ground and converted into gardens, pastures, and other uses.

Of the arches of triumph

The Romans used to edify certain arches and to dedicate them unto the names and memory of such as had conquered strange

[22] Baths of Caracalla, by the Appian Way.
[23] The Palatine; the reference is to the Circus Maximus.

countries or returned victoriously from dangerous battles; for the which they were received triumphantly into the city, sitting on a rich chariot drawn with four white steeds and their notable prisoners and spoil before them, with goodly representations of the gotten cities, towns, countries, and other things, and, so passing through the city, should ride unto the Temple of Jupiter in Capitolio.

There have been many of these arches, but at this day four only are to be known: that is, to wit, of Constantine, of Titus, of Severus, and of Domitian.

The first, of Constantine, standeth on the corner of the hill Palatinus, a little besides Coliseo, and is yet meetly fair to behold, were it not that the fine carved figures on both sides, wrought in the hard marble, are battered and almost defaced by the weather.

The next, of Titus and Vespasianus, is in the midst of the way called *Sacra*, wherein may be seen the representation of the chariot of triumph with the twelve sergeants on the one side and on the other the spoils of Jerusalem: that is, to wit, the golden candlestick of seven branches, the two tables of Moses, the golden table and vessel of the Temple, with divers other things, which, as Joseph [24] writeth, were laid up in the Temple of Peace.

The Arch of Septimius Severus standeth in the old market place,[25] now called *Piazza Romana*, at the foot of Campidoglio, and this is the fairest of all the other, having finely graven on both sides the representations of his battles and victories, as well by sea as by land, with the title in fair Roman letters to whom it was dedicated.

Finally, in the Way Flaminia, hard by the Church of St. Laurence in Lucina, is the Arch of Domitian,[26] as they say, and

---

[24] Josephus. [25] The Forum.
[26] The arch was actually that of Marcus Aurelius; it crossed the Corso (Via Flaminia) at the present Via delle Vite. It was called also *l'Arco di*

is now called *L'arco di Tripoli*—nothing of beauty comparable to any of the rest.

These arches are, as it were, gatehouses to pass through, but the fineness of the marble and curious workmanship showeth well that they were exceeding sumptuous and more beautiful than any other kind of building.

Of theaters

Like as the Romans in their wars, triumphs, and buildings exceeded all other nations of the world, even so did they in their feasts and spectacles: that is, to wit, in their plays and sights devised for pleasure and recreation.

One while they recited comedies; another while they used divers sounds of instruments to the *pantomimo*, who was one that with signs would counterfeit all manner of men and declare his conceit as evidently as if he should have spoken. Sometime they had a number of wild beasts brought in, as elephants, lions, tigers, and otherlike, against whom men that were either condemned to death, taken in the wars, or foolhardy fellows thereunto hired, should be put to fight and torn to pieces unless their chance were wonderful. Sometime again, the masters of fence with their scholars, and many times the soldiers, would enter with their sharp swords and there kill one another to try themselves valiant. Sometime they wrestled, sometime they jousted, and sometime they fought as it were in plain battle, as well by water as by land, with otherlike pastimes too long here to rehearse.

To behold these things, at the beginning every man took such place as he could get, but in process of years when their commonwealth flourished, then they devised certain scaffolds of board with grices or steps one above another and fastened them on great beams, made after the form of an half circle, for the

---

Portogallo, since the Portuguese embassy was nearby. The arch was taken down in 1662.

commodity of the more number of people to sit upon. Whereof Pliny saith thus: "Behold, the people—conqueror of other countries and lord of all the world; they that overthrow realms and nations, give law to strangers, and be, as it were, a certain divine thing amongst the human generation—stand here nevertheless, dangerously on an engine, rejoicing while they be in peril."

This engine of timber was called "theater," and the first that ever made any in Rome was Marcus Scaurus,[27] whose theater received fourscore thousand persons and served for thirty days only. But to ease the great charges that the building of such theaters required from time to time, Pompeius builded one of square stone,[28] sufficient for 80,000 persons; which theater Nero, at the receiving of Tiridates, King of Armenia, caused to be gilt clean over in a day.

Many of these theaters have been in Rome, but the most notable were these three of Pompeius, of Marcellus, and of Cornelius Balbus, of which there remaineth so little memory at this day that almost no man can tell where they stood.[29]

Finally, the Amphitheater, now called *Coliseo*, is yet standing, one of the perfectest to be seen amongst all the antiquities of Rome, and may indeed be accompted one of the wonders of the world. For though part of it be already fallen down and the rest decaying daily, yet is it not so defaced but that you may see perfectly what it hath been, as well for the marvelous height, great circuit, and fair stone, as also for the excellent workmanship and proportion. It is round both without and within; from the ground within upwards it riseth uniformly one step above

[27] In the Campus Martius.
[28] East of the present Piazza dei Fiori, under the Palazzo Pio-Righetti and nearby (Giuseppe Lugli [*I monumenti antichi di Roma e suburbio*, Rome, 1938], III, 70–83).
[29] The Theater of Marcellus on the Tiber was made over into the Palazzo Orsini, but it was marked with its original name on the Du Pérac map of 1577. The Theater of Cornelius Balbus was close by and some vestiges of it were still visible in Thomas' time.

35

another, stairwise, to a very great height, so that to behold the show in the bottom, which I think is above 300 yards in compass, there might sit an hundred thousand persons at their ease. And because they used to gravel the ground when any great pastime should be, therefore in the Latin tongue some authors have called it *Arena,* notwithstanding they have known the name to be *Amphitheatrum,* which signifieth two theaters joined together; and after most opinions this Amphitheater was builded by Vespasian and his son Titus.

There is also another Amphitheater yet to be seen, edified by Statilius Taurus,[30] but it is so decayed that it scarcely deserveth to be spoken of.

Of the circles [31]

As for the circles, which served to like purposes of spectacles, because there is none of them at this day that hath any similitude of their ancient being, I can say nothing to them.

Of the porches [32]

Of the solemn and sumptuous porches or vaults that many authors write were made through all the principal streets of Rome to cover the people from sun and rain, there be none now anything like, neither for the pillars nor yet for the proportion. Where is the porch of Nero that, Tranquillus[33] writeth, extended forthright 3,000 paces? Where be the porches of Livia, of Octavius and of his sister Octavia, of Pompeius, of Severus, and of many others? Amongst all of that sort there is but one remaining, which standeth before the door of the Temple Pantheon, situated on sixteen wonderful fair pillars set in three rows.

[30] This had long since disappeared. Thomas evidently referred instead to what is now identified as the Amphitheatrum Castrense or barracks theater, adjoining Santa Croce in Gierusalemme, and marked "Collosseum" on the Du Pérac map.
[31] Circuses.   [32] Both porticoes and arcades.
[33] Suetonius (C. Suetonius Tranquillus).

Description of Rome

Of temples

The Temple of Pantheon is the perfectest of all the antiquities and standeth whole unto this day. It is round and hath but one gate to enter in at; the doors whereof are of brass, very great and antique. The circuit withinforth is very large, and the height proportionable. The roof is all vaulted like the half of an egg, of so great compass that it is a wonder to behold, and in the very top is a great round hole, through which the Temple receiveth light. For other window it hath none, and yet is the light so much that if all the sides were made in windows it could give no more; under the which, in midst of the floor, is such hollow provision made that the rain passeth away without offending the eye or the place. Finally, the walls are furnished round about with fair marble and a number of goodly pillars, so that the Temple, being old, is yet thought goodlier than any new building that can be found and is now called *Santa Maria Rotonda*.

Many other temples have been in Rome that for the most part are likewise converted into churches, which to describe should be an endless work. But because of the alteration and ruin that time hath wrought, their true antiquity cannot be declared. Wherefore I will show where some stood and into what churches some other have been converted.

The ancient Temple of Romulus is now called *Santi Cosma e Damiano*, not much unlike the building of Pantheon, with the porch before and the gates likewise of brass. The ruin of the Temple of Peace, which was the beautifullest and richest of all the world, is yet to be seen between Palatine and Esquiline.[34] The Temple of Janus,[35] which was never open but in time of war, was near unto the church now called *San Giorgio in*

[34] The contemporary misnomer (as on the Du Pérac map) for the Basilica of Constantine, in the Forum. The Temple of Peace had been built beyond and above it, toward the Torre dei Conti.
[35] Still visible as the Arco di Jano.

Velabro. The Temple of Isis is now called *Santa Maria in Aquiro.*[36] The Temple of Minerva is now a house of friars called *Santa Maria sopra la Minerva.* And the Temple of Pallas was in the place before the Porch of Faustina, now called *Pallara.*[37]

As for the Temples of Fortune and Concord, which were many, besides a number of temples dedicated to the other gods and goddesses, there is none now worthy to be seen.

Of the pillars

It shall be necessary to declare that there be three kind of pillars: round, square, and striped. These are always of one piece, and the chapiter of the pillar, called in Latin *epistylium,* is the stone that standeth on the top of the pillar, like as the base, called *basis* in Latin, is the stone that the pillar standeth on. Of which bases there be four sundry fashions: *Ionici, Dorici, Italici,* and *Corinthii*—or *Tusculani,* as Vitruvius writeth. These kinds of pillars were so common amongst the Romans that almost he was no man that had not a number of pillars in his house of white, red, or divers colored marble, or of porphyry or otherlike rich stone, for the gray is not accompted marble in Italy but gray stone. So that to consider the infinite number of these pillars that were in Rome and that yet amongst the old ruins are to be seen, it seemeth a wonder where they should be had and what a treasure they cost. For I have seen divers almost two fathom about and above forty foot high. And nothing more earnestly desired I than to see some of those wonderful temples or edifices upon pillars in their old fashion, with the presence of some of

[36] The church is between the Pantheon and the Piazza Colonna.

[37] *Pallara* (or *Palladio,* from *palatium*) apparently meant to Thomas the area between the Forum and the Palatine. The Church of S. Maria in Pallara is equated by Armellini with that of S. Sebastiano, then above the Arch of Constantine, and Pallara seems actually to have meant the Palatine area. The Temple of Pallas (or Minerva) was in fact above the Forum on the other side, toward the Forum of Nervi, below the Torre dei Conti.

those ancient Romans that with their naked majesty durst pass through the power of their victorious enemies, as Livy writeth that Caius Fabius did when the Frenchmen [38] had gotten Rome and besieged the Capitol. But, to my purpose.

Besides these pillars of one stone, they used in Rome certain pillars called *structiles* that were made of divers stones. These were dedicated to the perpetual memory of the worthy emperors, as the two that yet stand do well witness.

The one is called the Pillar of Trajan, which is 123 foot high and hath a stair of 185 steps withinforth, whereby I have gone to the top. It hath forty-five little windows that give light inward, and is all of white marble, so well and finely graven with the stories of all Trajan's wars and victories that it should seem impossible to paint a thing better.

The other pillar, dedicated unto Antoninus Pius, much after the same sort hath his wars and doings set forth in figures graven, and is sixty-three foot higher but much more decayed than Trajan's pillar, for it is cleft almost from the top to the base, so that if it be not looked unto the sooner (as I think it shall not) it must needs fall.

There was such another pillar made all of porphyry, which Constantine took down and carried to Constantinople. Besides divers other pillars, as one of Caesar, another called *Milliarium Aureum, Moenia,* and *Lactaria,* and many mo, whereof no part remaineth now that can be known.

Of obelisks

Obeliscus is a stone that, being broad and square at the foot, ascendeth proportionally to a sharp point. Of which sort of stones there be but eight now to be seen in Rome, notwithstanding that Fulvius affirmeth there have been six great and forty-two small.

These obelisks were first invented by the Egyptians and dedi-

[38] The Gauls.

cated to the sun, not only because it hath the likeness of the sunbeam, but also because they used by the shadow thereof to try divers conclusions of astronomy, and specially the hours of the day, as by divers caracts [39] and figures that are yet seen in some of them it doth evidently appear.

And a wonder it is to think what an unreasonable enterprise it was to dig one of them out of the mountain, seeing it could not be had but by cutting away all the ground and rock about it.

In effect, there is but one of them standing, which is in the Vatican on the south side of St. Peter's Church, called *la Guglia*,[40] being seventy-two foot high of the very stone itself, besides the base and four great lions of marble that it is set upon, and hath on the top a great ball of brass gilt, with the ashes of Caesar in it, as some hold opinion. Octavian August brought two very great ones from Heliopolis in Egypt; the one whereof, being 122 foot high, brake in two pieces as they would have erected it, and the other, of 110 foot, lieth in Campo Marzio.[41] There lieth one in Girolo, that sometime was Sallustius' garden,[42] and two other lie beside the Church of St. Roch,[43]

[39] Carvings.

[40] A variant of *l'aguglia*, needle. The obelisk formerly south of St. Peter's was moved to the piazza, where it now is, in 1586.

[41] The obelisk in the Campus Martius, erected by Augustus to serve as the giant pointer of a sundial laid out in the square, was found buried there in Thomas' time. It was set up in the late eighteenth century in the Piazza Montecitorio, before the present palace of Parliament. The other obelisk from Heliopolis was one of two in the Circus Maximus, neither of which Thomas mentions. It is now in the Piazza del Popolo.

[42] *Lo Girolo* was a circus in the Varian Gardens at the Porta Maggiore, on the far side of Rome from the Gardens of Sallust, which are near the Pincian Gate. Actually, obelisks were discovered, in Thomas' time, in both gardens, and it is not possible to tell which one he refers to. The Varian obelisk is now in the Pincian gardens, and the Sallustian obelisk stands at the head of the Spanish Steps.

[43] On the river, close to the Mausoleum of Augustus, then closed in with houses. Two obelisks adorned the Mausoleum, and presumably these were the two referred to. One was taken to the Piazza Esquilina in 1587, behind S. Maria Maggiore; the other in 1786 to the Quirinal.

the one of them in the highway. The other two are but small and seem rather pieces than whole stone; the one is in the garden of Ara Coeli in the Capitol and the other is in the street of San Macuto.[44]

Of pyramids

There is no more pyramids in Rome but one, which the common people take to be the sepulcher of Remus, but the letters graven therein witness it to be the sepulcher of Caius Cestius, one of the seven men that was ordained over the feasts of the solemn sacrifices.[45] And whereas Livy writeth that Remus was buried in the hill Aventine, whereof it was named *Remuria*, it is manifest that this pyramid was not his sepulcher, for it standeth in the plain and in the very wall of the city between the gate of San Paolo and the hill Testaccio. The fashion of it is like unto a pointed diamond, and [it] is made of square stone, so great at the foot that, ascending uniformly to the top, it is higher than any tower of the wall.

In the highways without the city, specially Flaminia, Salaria, and Appia, be many like seen of much less quantity, but for the most part they are either decayed or decaying—like as the *cimiteri*, which were vaults under earth that served of later time for Christian sepultures, which, with otherlike kind of buildings, by process of years are worn and come to naught.

Of Colosses and images

Colossus signifieth an unreasonable great image, such as that of Apollo that was brought out of Apollonia in Pontus and set in the Capitol, whose height was thirty cubits, or that of Jupiter in Campo Marzio, commonly called *Pompeianus*. But above all that ever were, the Colossus at Rhodes exceeded. For it was

[44] Close behind the Piazza Colonna; the Du Pérac map shows the small obelisk. It is now in the square before the Pantheon.
[45] The *septemviri* organized the banquets on religious holidays.

seventy cubits high and so proportionate to that height that, lying on the earth (after it was shaken down by an earthquake),
few men could embrace one of the fingers, and many of the
hollow places in the joints seemed valleys or deep bottoms; so
that it is written the Saracens, after they had gotten Rhodes,
laded above 900 camels with the brass that they picked out of
that Colossus.

Nero caused one to be made of 120 foot high to his own likeness and set it in the porch of his golden house, which afterwards was removed thence unto the Amphitheater, and thereof
it is thought it took the name of Coliseo.

Finally, I can find no more of these Colosses whole at this day,
but one head, one hand, and a foot that lie before the doors of
the Conservatori in the Capitol.

It is true that in many places of Rome are seen wonderful
pieces of marble that should seem to have been members of
those Colosses, but they are in manner clean defaced.

Likewise, of the excellent images, both of brass and marble,
as well of men as of horse, many pieces yet remain, though
scarcely worth the name of good images as they appear now.

Fulvius writeth that there were in Rome twenty-four horses of
brass gilt and 114 of ivory, besides a number of men's images on
horseback and on foot of marble and other matter. But of all
these there are now none to be seen, saving one of brass on
horseback at St. John Lateran,[46] which some ascribe unto
Marcus Aurelius Antoninus, some to Lucius Verus, and some to
Severus, and another there is in the Capitol called *il Gran'
Villano.*[47]

[46] It had been transferred to the Capitol by Pope Paul III.

[47] *Gran' villano* (big peasant) was another name for the Marcus Aurelius
statue, which in medieval legend was said to honor a rustic who had
saved Rome. (I owe this identification to the kindness of Dr. Phyllis Pray
Bober, director of the Census of Antique Works of Art.) Thomas evidently
saw the statue at the Capitol, where it had been moved in 1538; but the

Description of Rome

Indeed, there be divers bodies without heads; I think because some strangers, delighting in those antiquities, have broken off the heads to carry them away.

Amongst all other, Constantius, son of Constantine, being come out of Greece to see Rome and arrived in the street called *Forum Traiani*, rested all amazed to behold the wonderful beauty thereof and, despairing with himself to be able to bring to pass any of those things that were before his eyes, said he would see whether he could make such another horse of brass as was there under Trajan in the midst of the market place. Whereunto one of his skillful men present, named Ormisda, answered that he were best first to make such another stable to put his horse in. And if emperors themselves have marveled at these things, why should not other men wonder at them?

Of the hill Testaccio

If the common report be true, this hill is one of the notablest things amongst the antiquities of Rome, because (as they say) the Romans ordained that all tributes which were brought yearly to Rome should be laid in pots made of the earth of the countries from whence it came; which pots, after the money was paid, should be brought to the place where this hill lieth, there to be broken and remain on an heap for a perpetual memory of the Roman Empire. And being well considered, it shall appear that there can be no device like unto this to have a thing endure forever. For if the hill had been made of any matter worth the carrying away, it should have been spoiled long ere this time, but because there is nothing to be gotten, saving potsherds, therefore it remaineth whole as none other antiquity doth. And

---

books still located the Marcus Aurelius at the Lateran, and Thomas made two statues out of one. If he had gone inside the Capitol museum, he would have seen more statues.

although learned men allow not this vulgar opinion, thinking it hath grown rather of the broken pots that have been thrown out of the seventh college of potters [48] founded by Numa Pompilius, yet beholding advisedly the place whereon it standeth, being the fairest plain within the walls of Rome, meseemeth it half incredible that the Romans would suffer so fair a ground to be occupied with potsherds unless there were some further purpose in it than I can imagine. For the hill is little lack of half a mile compass, higher a great deal than any tower in the town wall, and so easy to get up on every side that I have ridden up at the one end and down at the other, and yet is the earth of it so thin that, digging three inches deep, you shall find potsherds.

De Hippodromo

Between this Testaccio and the hill Aventine is a fair green, anciently called *Hippodromus*, where some years at Shrovetide the Romans use to this day to tourney on horseback; and among other pastimes they tie two bulls to the tail of a cart and so drive the cart from the top of Testaccio down into the plain, and he that first can take the cart and bulls shall have them. But if the bulls break loose, as many times they do, they make foul work amongst the people ere they be taken, so that sometimes they are fain to kill them. Some hold opinion that this play was first devised by Tarquinius Priscus to be celebrated in February in honor of the infernal gods.

Of graners and arsenals

On the other side, between Testaccio and Tiber, have been 140 graners for corn, long and large, as by some of the old foundations it doth yet appear. And somewhat nearer the foot

---

[48] The mythical college (or guild) of potters was suggested by Biondo. It is now understood that broken vessels which had brought in foodstuffs from the provinces to the port of Rome were required to be dumped here behind the granaries along the shore.

of the hill Aventine were the cellars and vaults for salt and all manner of merchandise, with the arsenals where their ships and galleys were made, of which at this day is scarce any sign to be perceived.

Finally, it were too tedious a matter for me to speak of every notable thing in Rome. For if Blondus nor yet Fulvius, Italians born, dwelling in Rome and well-learned men, have travailed therein and would not yet undertake fully to describe those antiquities, should I, a stranger, that tarried there but a small time, enterprise to do it? And yet amongst all other I had almost forgotten the sepulcher of Bacchus,[49] that lieth in a little old temple beside the Church of St. Agnes-without-the-Walls, more notable for the value of the stone than for the workmanship. For it is of fine red porphyry, plain and square like a chest, and so great that the only cover would require a great force to lift it up; so that my guide said merrily if I had company sufficient to raise up this stone I would one night see what were within, meaning that the god Bacchus could not be buried there without some treasure.

And to the intent that generally men may the better understand the sorts of marble and manners of building wherewith the city hath been anciently beautified, I shall here rehearse one saying of Fulvius:

The ancient great buildings, as well public as private, for the most part were founded upon great square stones, to the end that the weight and substance of the building should be the more steadfast, every stone so joined to other with iron clasps that they needed no mortar. And then the wall from the foundation upwards was made of stones that weighed not past a pound weight apiece, laid together proportionally checkerwise. The front of the building was most commonly wrought after the manner of a net or pargetted [50] either with

---

[49] Now known to be the tomb of St. Constantia, daughter of Constantine, in the mausoleum which is now the Church of Santa Costanza.

[50] Plastered. The passage is from Fulvio, book V, fol. c.

a fair white mixture or else with jesse,[51] and some covered finely with thin marble or with certain plates of latten gilt.[52] The vaults and roofs of the chambers were trimmed either with glass, with lead, with jesse, or else with very fine paintings, and the floors underfoot made some of glass and some of the finest marble or other pleasant devices of divers making.

They had many kinds of strange marble, as white marble of the Isle of Paros and of Carrara, and that which cometh from Laconia the pleasantest of all; the red marble not unlike the masard,[53] with certain white spots, which they call porphyry; the bloody marble that groweth in Troad; the black marble called *luculleus;* the spotted marble called serpentine; the onyx brought out of Arabia; the alabaster and some marble transparent that is to be seen through, as the phengite,[54] with divers others.

Of the Present State of Rome

OF THE ground contained within the walls scarcely the third part is now inhabited, and that not where the beauty of Rome hath been but for the most part on the plain to the waterside and in the Vatican, because that since the Bishops began to reign every man hath coveted to build as near the court as might be. Nevertheless, those streets and buildings that are there at this time are so fair that I think no city doth excel it, by reason they have had the beautifullest things of the antiquities before rehearsed to garnish their houses withal, specially the Bishop, his cardinals, prelates, and other members of his church, who have all at their commandment. For though the Romans have in their

[51] Gesso (plaster or gypsum).   [52] A brass alloy (Italian *ottone*).
[53] I do not identify "masard"; the original says only "red decorated with white spots."
[54] Probably gypsum.

46

hearts unto this day a certain memory of their ancient liberty, which they have attempted many times to recover, yet doth the Bishop keep them in such subjection that they dare not once stir for their lives, but speak they may what they list, so it be no treason; and therefore many times you shall hear them rail on the Bishop and his officers that it is a wonder. In effect, the present state of Rome in comparison of the ancient state deserveth not to be spoken of, and yet I believe that in the Romans' most glory there was never half so much pomp used as now. O what a world it is to see the pride and abomination that the churchmen there maintain! What is a king? what is an emperor in his majesty? anything like to the Roman Bishop? No, surely no; I would not wish them so to be. And to the intent you may the better perceive it, you shall understand that on Christmas Day the year of our Lord 1547, Paul the Third being Bishop, I noted his coming to church because it was a principal feast celebrated *in pontificalibus.* Wherefore early in the morning I resorted to the palace and there waited the coming of the cardinals, that for the most part lie in the city and to come to St. Peter's must pass Ponte Sant' Angelo; where is an old order that whensoever any cardinal passeth the bridge there is a piece of ordnance shot off in the castle for an honor that the Bishop is bound to observe towards his brethren.

I had not been long in the palace but I heard two pieces shot off at once, whereby I knew that two cardinals were coming, and therefore resorted to the gate to see them and their train.

From Castel Sant' Angelo to St. Peter's stairs there is an exceeding fair street, straight and level more than a quarter of a mile long, called *Borgo San Pietro;* in the further end whereof I saw these cardinals come, and therewith out of the Bishop's palace came his guard of Switzers all in white harness and there alongst before the gate made a lane half on one side and half on the other, with their two drums and a fife before them. And as soon as the cardinals approached, the drums and fife began to

47

play and so continued till the cardinals were well entered amongst the guard. Then the trumpets blew up another while till the cardinals were almost at the gate, and as they should enter, the shawms began to play and ceased not till they were alighted and mounted up the stairs to the Bishop's lodging.

The like ceremonies were used unto all the cardinals that came, whether one came alone or many together. And there [I] tarried more than two hours, hearkening to this gunshot and merry piping, and reckoned above forty cardinals that came thus riding, sometime one alone and sometime three or four together.

There was no cardinal that came without a great train of gentlemen and prelates, well horsed and appointed—some had forty, some fifty, and some sixty or more—and next before every of them rode two henchmen, the one carrying a cushion and a rich cloth, and the other a pillar of silver; and the cardinals themselves, appareled in robes of crimson chamlet[1] with red hats on their heads, rode on mules.

When they were all come to the palace and had waited awhile in the chamber of presence, the Bishop himself, with the three-crowned miter full of jewels, in a very rich cope, with shoes of crimson velvet set with precious stones, and in all his other pontifical apparel, came forth and at the chamber door sat him down in a chair of crimson velvet, through the which runneth two staves covered with the same. Thus being set, the prelates and clergy with the other officers passed on afore him; which are such a number as were able to make the muster of a battle if they were well ordered in the field: dataries, treasurers, clerks of the chamber, penitentiaries, prebendaries, notaries, protonotaries, and a thousand mo, each order of them in his divers device of parliament robes, all in scarlet and for the most part finely furred. Then came the double cross, the sword, and

[1] Originally camel hair; now probably wool and silk.

the imperial hat, and after that the cardinals by two and two, and between every two a great rout of gentlemen. Then came the ambassadors and next them the Bishop himself, blessing all the way and carried in his chair by eight men, clothed in long robes of scarlet; and on either side of him went his guard, making room and crying, *Abbasso, Abbasso,* for they that will not willingly kneel shall be made kneel by force. And I think verily the foremost of this order was distant from the hindermost more than a quarter of a mile.

Thus when he came into the midst of the church against the sacrament of the altar, he turned himself towards it and, bowing his head a little, seemed to make a certain familiar reverence. Then was he carried into the chapel, brought behind the altar (for the altar standeth in the midst, open every way), and there in a throne of wonderful majesty was set up as a god.

The cardinals then bestowed themselves after their ancienty in certain stalls, somewhat lower about the choir. Then sat the ambassadors and other prelates at their feet. And so when they were set, the chapel began the Offertory of the Mass and sang so sweetly that methought I never heard the like. At the communion of the Mass, the cardinal that celebrated brake the host in three pieces, whereof he eat one himself, and the other two he delivered upon the paten to a cardinal appointed that brought it to the Bishop, and in his presence (for fear of poisoning) took assay of the second piece and delivered him the third. When the Mass was finished, the Bishop gave his benediction, with many years of pardon, and then returned to the palace in like order as he came.

As for the pomp he useth when he rideth abroad, I need not to speak of it, considering what I have said, saving that you shall understand how Corpus Domini is always carried in a tabernacle before him on a white hackney that is taught to kneel both at the setting up and also at the taking down of it.

Indeed, the Bishop for his own ordinary keepeth no great house, but his train exceedeth all that I have seen. For every cardinal and prelate keepeth house according to his ability, and some of them are so precise that if one of their retinue be missing when they go out of their doors, be it gentleman or other, he forfeiteth a certain piece of money, which he is constrained forthwith to pay. And lightly there is none of them without three or four pages trimmed like young princes, for what purpose I would be loath to tell.

If I should say that under their long robes they hide the greatest pride of the world, it might happen some men would believe it, but that they are the vainest men of all other their own acts do well declare. For their ordinary pastime is to disguise themselves, to go laugh at the courtesans' houses, and in the shroving time to ride masking about with them; which is the occasion that Rome wanteth no *jolie dames,* specially the street called *Julia,* which is more than half a mile long, fair builded on both sides, in manner inhabited with none other but courtesans, some worth 10 and some worth 20,000 crowns, more or less, as their reputation is. And many times you shall see a courtesan ride into the country with ten or twelve horses waiting on her.

Briefly, by report Rome is not without 40,000 harlots, maintained for the most part by the clergy and their followers. So that the Romans themselves suffer their wives to go seldom abroad, either to church or other place, and some of them scarcely to look out at a lattice window; whereof their proverb saith, *In Roma vale piu la putana che la moglie Romana:* that is to say, "In Rome the harlot hath a better life than she that is a Roman's wife."

In their apparel they are as gorgeous as may be and have in their going such a solemn pace as I never saw. In conclusion, to live in Rome is more costly than in any other place, but he that hath money may have there what him liketh. But now remaineth to speak of the new buildings.

Of St. Peter's Church

The Church of St. Peter standeth somewhat aloft on the hill Vatican and hath before it a very fair and large room, as it were a market place, in the midst whereof is a goodly fountain of marble that gusheth out water of a great height.

From this place up to the church are about thirty steps or grices of square stone, the solemnest that I have seen, for they are almost thirty paces long. At the top of this stair over the midst of a goodly porch is a great image of St. Peter of fine marble. Within that is a large court paved with fine marble, in the midst whereof is an antique pineapple [2] of brass of a wonderful bigness, and so many images, pillars, and other rich stones that have been gathered out of the antiquities and brought thither to furnish the new buildings withal that it should be an endless work to describe them. Out of this court is the entry into the church, which hath three great gates of brass, wherein the stories of the acts of Eugenius the Fourth [3] are finely graven.

This church within is nothing fair to the eye, but it hath in it many beautiful and fine things, as the tabernacle of marble where, they say, Christ's sudary and one of the three nails lieth, the goodly brazen sepulture of Sixtus the Fourth, the brazen images of St. Peter and Paul, a number of goodly pillars, and divers other things.

But above all, the new building, if it were finished, would be the goodliest thing of this world, not only for the antique pillars that have been taken out of the antiquities and bestowed there, but also for the greatness and excellent good proportion that it hath. Nevertheless, it hath been so many years adoing and is

[2] Pine cone (Italian *pigna*). This Roman bronze, eleven feet high, is now in the Cortile della Pigna in the Vatican grounds.

[3] Pope, 1431–1447. The inscriptions, and the doors on which they were carved, disappeared when the façade of old St. Peter's was removed before 1615, when the new church, begun in 1506, replaced the old.

yet so imperfect that most men stand in doubt whether ever it shall be finished or no.

In the midst of this new building is a pretty chapel, wherein the Bishop with all his cardinals and clergy use to celebrate their solemn ceremonies.

Of the Bishop's palace with Belvedere

The Bishop's palace joineth to the church, which to mine eye seemeth much greater than goodly, notwithstanding the lodgings withinforth are fair, but I can most commend the stair that goeth down from the palace to the church, almost a quarter of a mile about, so fair paved and plain that a man may easily ride up and down.

About three quarters of a mile from the palace is the Bishop's banqueting house, called Belvedere, one of the finest buildings that is to be seen, so rich, so pleasant, and of so goodly a prospect that it seemeth almost another paradise. The garden walled round about is full of fair orange trees and hath in the midst a goodly fountain with perfect plots in mold of the river of Nile in Egypt and of Tiber that runneth through Rome, besides the images of fine marble of Romulus and Remus playing with a wolf's teats, of Apollo with his bow and arrows, of *Laocoònte* with his two children wrapped about with serpents, of Venus beholding little Cupido, of the sorrowful Cleopatra lying by the riverside, and of divers other too long to rehearse.

Of Castel Sant' Angelo

This castle is no less notable than some of the rest. It standeth on the bank of Tiber in manner clean without the town and hath three wards, one within another, excellently well builded and strong, and after most men's opinions is impregnable, unless it be by famine. The two inner wards stand upon the sepulcher of the Emperor Hadrian, which is a certain black mass of earth of a great height, compounded of certain mixtures, which being dried is harder and more durable than stone itself. Upon this foundation Hadrian made his tomb and decked it with such ornaments of marble and other sumptuous things as made it seem one of the rarest things of the world. But after it came to the Bishops' hands, considering the force of the place and strong foundation, they converted it into a fortress and have edified many goodly lodgings upon it, so that oftentimes the Bishop himself lieth in it and keepeth his court there.

Of buildings in general

Finally, there be a number of as fair palaces in Rome as in any other place of the world, whereof it should be too long here to make particular mention, but specially the palace that Paul, now Bishop, there hath builded by the place called *Campo di Fiori,* where Pompeius' house stood in the old time, deserveth not to be forgotten. For he hath rooted out of the ruins of the antiquities such goodly marble pillars and other fine stone which he hath bestowed on that house that if he finish it as it is begun it will be the gallantest thing, old or new, that shall be found again in all Europe, and he hath called it after his own name, *Palazzo Farnese.*

Abridgment of the Lives of the Roman Bishops

BECAUSE my principal purpose tendeth to describe the states of Italy, I need not to use much circumstance either in matters of religion or yet in writing all the lives of the Bishops of Rome. Wherefore, intending to begin at Sylvester, the first Bishop there that had anything in perpetuity, I have thought good to declare the divers opinions of their original.

Some ancient authors affirm that Peter, one of Christ's apostles, after that he had sufficiently confirmed the Church in Asia and confuted the error of those Christians that allowed circumcision, came to Rome the second year of Claudius' empire and there was received of the congregation as Bishop. In which office he ministered twenty-five years, and at last was crucified with the head downwards, the same day that Paul the apostle was beheaded, the last year of Nero's reign and the thirty-seventh year after Christ's death.

Contrariwise, many learned men at these days are of opinion that Peter never came in Rome, grounding themselves upon divers reasons as this: If Peter had comen thither, it could not have been unwritten in the Holy Scriptures, either by Luke in the Acts of the Apostles or else by Paul in some of his Epistles. Or if Peter were of that age that it should seem he was at Christ's death, and after continued in Antioch and other places so many years as is to be proved, it seemeth impossible he should come to Rome and there live twenty-five years. Wherefore they say the ambitious Bishops of Rome, to cover their usurped authority, have feigned this coming of Peter thither.

But this is clear, that from Peter to Sylvester they reckon thirty-three Bishops, which for the most part were persecuted and many of them martyred by the Emperor's officers. So that in manner they always kept themselves out of sight, preaching and ministering secretly without pomp, state, or solemn ceremony. But from the time of Sylvester hitherwards, as they grew in wealth so increased their worldly majesty and ambition, as hereafter more plainly appeareth.

As for the Bishops' names, the time of their reign, and the date of our Lord, because that in a table I have put them all together, I need not particularly to rehearse every one of them but such as the occasion of my purpose shall necessarily require.

Sylvester, the first of that name, after he had been a certain space in the hill Soratte,[1] now called *Monte di San Silvestro,* where for fear of persecution he hid himself, hearing of the good inclination that the Emperor Constantine the First was of toward Christian religion, came to Rome and so discreetly behaved himself that the Emperor was converted to the right faith and baptized.

Some write that the occasion thereof proceeded of a miracle done on Constantine in recovering his health from the leprosy. But Platina thinketh that to be a fable and in manner proveth it, thinking rather it proceeded of the sign of the cross that Constantine did see in the firmament under which he was promised victory, and so, carrying a red cross in his standard before him, he overcame his enemy Maxentius, whereupon he gave ear to Sylvester's preaching and was converted. But whatsoever the occasion was, it is agreed that Sylvester baptized Constantine, who, being christened, turned many of the Gentiles' temples to Christian churches, enduing them with ornaments and possessions.

Not long after, leaving Rome to Sylvester and his successors, as the clergy say, Constantine went to dwell at Byzantium, which he had then newly re-edified, calling it Constantinople after his own name. So that from thenceforth the Christian faith began to flourish over all the world, and therefore most part of all Christian churches sent to the Bishops of Rome to learn of them the ceremonies and orders necessary to be used in the church, by reason whereof—the Emperors being resident elsewhere—the Roman bishops grew in such reputation that at length they became emperors themselves.

And there is an ancient writing in the Vatican Library called the "Donation of Constantine," which is so vehement liberal that it should seem the Emperor spoiled himself of all his glory and honor and of a great part of his dominion to give them to the

[1] The Roman Mt. Soracte, some fifty miles north of Rome.

Church of Rome; by authority whereof the Roman bishops have taken upon them the imperial vestments, majesty, commandments, and dominion over some countries.

Indeed, Laurentius Valla, an excellent learned man and a Roman born, hath written a book [2] to confound this Donation of Constantine and proveth by so many reasons that it hath been feigned by some Bishop of later time than Sylvester that I am persuaded rather to believe him than the Donation. In effect, this Sylvester was the first that prescribed a direct order of ministers in the Church and how they should be known in their degrees from the highest to the lowest; by whose time there sprung divers sects amongst the Christians, as the Arians, Photines, Sabellians, and others, for whose reformation the Nicene Council was called, but for all that those errors ceased not many years after.

[We omit here the chronicle of the Popes, which takes up some 58 pages more (ff. 43–72v), and give only the last 7½ pages concerning the Popes since 1494.]

Alexander the Sixth [3] was a Spaniard born and a great philosopher. He entered in league with Alfonso, King of Naples, against Charles the Eighth, French king, who then prepared himself to come into Italy.

Nevertheless, Charles's power was such that the Bishop not only gave him passage but also received him in Rome honorably. And yet, mistrusting the French king's high courage, seeing he feared but little the ecclesiastical power, the Bishop withdrew himself into Castel Sant' Angelo, though by fair entreaty he came out again and yielded all his dominion at the King's will,

---

[2] *De falso credita et ementita Constantini donatione declamatio,* written 1439 and published 1517. It had recently (1534) been published in English as an antipapal argument.

[3] Alessandro Borgia.

and, besides that, delivered him Zizimo, brother to the Great Turk, that before was the Bishop's prisoner.[4]

But ere ever Charles returned out of the realm of Naples, which was within less than half a year after, the Bishop had wrought a new league against him wherein the Emperor Maximilian, the King of Aragon, the Venetians, and the Duke of Milan were his colleagues; so that Charles in his return toward France was fought withal and sore handled.

Finally, Charles being thus departed, this Bishop began to wax high, and imagining how to extol his own name, he created his son Valentino Borgia [5] Duke, causing him first to renounce his cardinal hat, which at his father's creation was given him, and then made he him captain of an army sent into Romagna, where first he warred against Katherine,[6] lady of Imola and Forlì, and not only took her just possessions from her but also sent her prisoner to Rome, and then proceeded further against the other lords thereabouts. So that having chased away the families of Manfredi, Ordelaffi, Malatesta, Feltrani, Varani, and divers other, in manner of no less estate than princes, he gat into his possession the countries of Romagna and Marca d'Ancona, with the dukedoms of Urbino, Camerino, and Spoleto. Of all the which his father entitled him Duke,[7] and entered into so great a pride with his son's prosperity that he would say to him, "Either a Caesar or nothing."

Through comfort whereof, being given to overmuch covetousness, in hope of empire he poisoned divers rich cardinals to have their goods, and amongst his other practices he appointed poisoned comfits for a cardinal that dined with his father, but the father himself was served of the wrong box and died and the

---

[4] The brother of Sultan Bajazet had fled for safety to the West; the Pope accepted a large bribe from the Sultan to keep him prisoner and to have him murdered. He died in Charles's custody on the way to Naples.

[5] Cesare Borgia, Duke of Valentinois in France: hence the name Valentino in Italy.

[6] Caterina Sforza.   [7] Of Romagna.

57

son not long after slain in the midst of all his glory; [8] notwith-standing that by his father's time he was coupled in marriage with the daughter of the Duke of Ferrara.

Pius the Third died within a month, not without suspicion of venom. Julius the Second, being a man more given to arms than to prayer, more like Julius Caesar than Simon Peter, was wont to say that Maximilian had been meet to be Bishop and he Emperor.

First he procured such a league against the Venetians that they had never a foot of ground left them on the mainland; so that he had for his part Ravenna with the other cities of Romagna. He destroyed the family of Borgia and quieted much the civil sedition that had long time reigned in the Roman nobility. He made war against the Bentivogli, that then were lords of Bologna, and, having chased them away, entered into that city with like triumph as the ancient Roman conquerors were wont to do into Rome. Many times he would go armed himself, specially in the enterprise against Ludovicus Picus of Mirandola.[9]

Finally, fearing the French king's [10] too much prosperity, he entered in league with the Venetians and the King of Spain against the French king, which was occasion of the notable Battle of Ravenna, fought on Easter Day,[11] where on both sides were slain about 30,000 men. For as I have been credibly informed, when both battles were joined—Spaniards on the one side and Frenchmen on the other—the Duke of Ferrara, that came on the French part, shot off his artillery amongst the thickest and slew a multitude as well of his friends as enemies, but they were all strangers to him.

In conclusion, the Frenchmen took Ravenna with divers other

[8] In 1507, four years after his father's death—but in exile in France.
[9] The famous scholar Giovanni Pico (died 1494) was a younger son in the family of the lords of Mirandola.
[10] Louis the Twelfth.　　　　[11] In 1512.

cities of the Bishop's, which they enjoyed not long. For the Bishop immediately gat into his league the Emperor, the King of England, the Germans, and the Switzers. So that the French king, being vexed on all sides, was easily constrained to forgo his conquests and dominions in Italy, specially through force of the Switzers; that, under the leading of their Cardinal Sedunense,[12] came in great number to the Bishop's service, who rewarded them with the title of Defenders of the Church and gave them a gilt sword and an hat of maintenance.

Somewhat before his death he established his cousin, Francesco Maria, Duke of Urbino.

Leo the Tenth of the house of Medici, a Florentine born, was a pleasant man of nature and gave himself more to humanity and pleasures of this life than either to religion or to increase of dominion. He increased much the reputation of his house, but because he expulsed by force Francesco Maria, Duke of Urbino, out of his state and placed in the same, first, his brother Julian and, after, his nephew Laurence, the world accused him of tyranny. For he attempted to do the like unto the Duke of Ferrara, but he prevailed not. Some ill was suspected of him for his too much delicateness in bringing up of children and for his opinion of immortality.[13]

Adrian the Seventh,[14] by contention amongst the cardinals, happened to be elected, reputed of them for an ignorant man, though some other had a good opinion both of his virtue and learning. But because his life was nothing courtly or agreeable to the cardinals, either through God's visitation or, as most men think, through their poison practices, he was soon dispatched.

Clement the Seventh, brother unto Leo the Tenth, immedi-

---

[12] Matthew Cardinal Schinner, Bishop of Sion (Sedunense) in Switzerland, cardinal 1511–1522.

[13] That is, for his supposed lack of belief in immortality.

[14] An error for Adrian the Sixth. He was in fact not a compromise candidate but the one sponsored by the Emperor Charles the Fifth, whose subject he was, being Flemish.

ately after his election took part with the French king against the Emperor. So that when the French king was taken before Pavia,[15] the family of Colonna, which hath been always imperial, through help of Don Ugo de Moncada, began to war with the Bishop and, after divers subtle practices and persuasions, so handled the matter that they entered into Rome and missed but a little to have taken the Bishop, who, hearing the rumor, suddenly fled to Castel Sant' Angelo. Wherefore, after the Bishop had drawn Don Ugo de Moncada to his part, the Colonnesi endured cruel war to their great damage.

Then came the Duke of Bourbon, who was slain with the shot of an handgun from the walls of Rome, but the Emperor's army, whereof he was captain, took the city by assault, sacked, spoiled, and burned it,[16] and for the space of fifteen days used such triumph that for their pastime they would make such cardinals and prelates as were their prisoners ride scornfully about the town upon asses, with their faces to the tail, and so straitly besieged Clement that he was fain to give them 400,000 ducats for his ransom and to yield the castle into the Emperor's hands.

But within less than three years after, the Emperor came himself into Italy and, having made peace with the Bishop, received of him the imperial crown in Bologna, with so great triumph and pomp that the like hath not been heard of in our days. During the which there came ambassadors to Clement with letters from Prester John [17] of great commendations, desire of amity, and union of religion.

Before their departure from Bologna, the Emperor granted the Bishop his army against the Florentines and concluded the marriage of his bastard daughter to Clement's nephew, Alexander de' Medici, that afterwards was Duke of Florence. But ere the Florentines would lose their liberties, they sustained a notable war for the space of twelve months.

And like as by force he oppressed the Florentines, so by

[15] In 1525.   [16] In 1527.   [17] The Emperor of Abyssinia.

treason he subdued Ancona. For, under pretense of amity and counsel, persuading them that the Turks' army by sea was coming against them, he sent a captain of his called Bernardin,[18] who with certain men of war was received into the city and so usurped the dominion for the Church.

In this Bishop's time happened such a sudden rage of water in Rome that the high towers were drowned and a great number of people with infinite riches lost, so that the Bishop himself had much ado to escape it; which may well be thought a plague of God, sent for the abomination that reigneth there.

Finally, Clement met with the French king at Marseilles in Provence and there concluded the marriage that followed between Katherine,[19] Clement's niece, and Henry, now French king, then but second son to the French king; shortly after whose marriage Clement died.

Paul the Third, that now is Bishop, before the time of his election held himself so indifferent between the factions imperial and French that no man could know to whether part he was most inclined.

In the beginning of his time, he procured all Christian princes to war against the Turk so that the Emperor, the Venetians, and he made an army by sea under the leading of Andrea Doria, who met with Barbarossa beside Corfu, but they fought no battle though the Christians were more in number and better furnished than the Turks; whether Andrea Doria were blameworthy I cannot tell. But once the Venetian galleon, a notable ship, was left alone in the midst of the Turkish navy, that assaulted her four or five hours, and yet at length came clean away in despite of them all.

This Bishop went to Nice in Provence, where by his procurement the Emperor and French king met and concluded a peace, which dured not long.

[18] Bernardino Dellabarba, papal legate to the Marches.
[19] Caterina de' Medici, married to Henry the Second.

Then died the Duke of Urbino. Incontinently upon whose death the Bishop made war to the young Duke Guidobaldo for the state of Camerino and constrained him for a little sum of money to give over the state, in which the Bishop established his own son, Pietro Aluigi, Duke.

After this, upon a light occasion the Bishop made war to Ascanio Colonna, chief of that family; and Pietro Aluigi, being general of the Bishop's army, handled Ascanio Colonna and his adherents so cruelly that they were fain to abandon their own towns and castles and to live in exile as banished men till by the Emperor's means they were restored to the Bishop's favor and absolution.

This Paul, to exalt his own blood, by consent of his cardinals exchanged the duchy of Camerino with the church for the cities and territories of Piacenza and Parma. Whereof he invested his forenamed son as Duke, whose behavior was such that he continued not fully two years, for the nobility of the same, detesting his wicked life and tyranny, conspired against him and slew him in his own house in Piacenza, yielding that city the next day into the Emperor's hands.[20]

The Bishop sent a fair army both of horsemen and footmen to succor the Emperor in his enterprise against the Germans and made his son's son, called the Duke Ottavio, general.

Finally, he is a great astronomer and so old a man that (as they say) for the most part he is nourished with the suck of a woman's breasts and to help his cold nature hath two young girls to lie by him in his bed anights.

[Following the lives of the Popes, which end here, Thomas adds a chronology, which requires 5⅓ unnumbered pages (sigs. T–Tiiiv). We give the ending (sig. Tiiiv).]

[20] Pierluigi Farnese was assassinated in 1547, during Thomas' stay in Italy, as Thomas says later. His father, Paul the Third, died in November, 1549, while this book was presumably in press.

Anno Domini	Number of bishop	Names	Years	Months
1492	226	Alexander VI	11	
1503	227	Pius III		1
1503	228	Julius II	9	4
1513	229	Leo X	9	3
1522	230	Adrian VI	1	7
1523	231	Clement VII	11	
1535	232	Paul III	14	

Authors do vary somewhat in the times of these Bishops, but I have agreed the best together and so have set it forth.

The Venetian State

BECAUSE the marvelous situation of the city of Venice amongst other things seemeth unto me most notable, I therefore have thought good first to treat thereof and then consequently to proceed unto the declaration of the Venetian state, their customs, and proceedings.

Of the marvelous site

When I consider what things necessity causeth (having an earnest proof for my part thereof), I nothing marvel to see the wonders that it worketh. For he that beholdeth the place where Venice standeth and would imagine it to be without any building or habitation should say it were the rudest, unmeetest, and unwholesomest place to build upon or to inhabit that were again to be found throughout an whole world. It standeth open upon the main sea, four miles from the nearest mainland, in such a marsh as at every low water leaveth the muddy ground uncovered and at every full sea drowneth it clean. And yet men (constrained of necessity) have brought this marsh to such a pass that it is now not only exceeding full of people and rich of treasure and buildings but so wholesome withal (through the much haunt of people and the great number of continual fires) that I think none other city able to show so many old men. But were it not that, as it seemeth, nature hath of purpose made a bank two or three miles off between it and the sea, it were impossible to be inhabited because, the city standing equal with the water, the flood by reason should pass through the houses at every full sea. But this bank, that beginneth at Chiozza and stretcheth toward the city of Concordia, sixty miles of length, doth so defend the water flood that within those marshes it hath nothing the like force as on the other seacoasts. For it is a great matter when the sea swelleth in Venice four or five foot above the low-water mark, notwithstanding that the city seemeth to be rather in a part of the sea than in a marsh. For every channel [1] (as who should say every street) is full of water, and the channels are so many that you may row through all parts of the city, though there be ways also to go on land if you list. Which streets for the most part are very narrow and the houses nothing so fair as on the waterside. And in the marsh between the city and the mainland, when the water is low, the most part of the channels are so shallow that the boats have much ado to pass to and fro. For the mud increaseth daily by reason of the land floods that a number of rivers, falling into the same, do carry with them. And a wonderful treasure the Venetians spend in continual digging and carrying away of that mud to preserve their foresaid channels and to defend that their city join not to the mainland.

[1] Thomas translates *canale* as "channel," the established English word (from French *chenal*); so did Evelyn, a century later. "Canal" is a later re-translation.

The bank before rehearsed is broken in seven places, through the which boats may come in, but no ship can pass to Venice saving at the port of Malamocco or at the two castles of Lido. The entry whereof is so dangerous (by reason the sands are movable here and there) that when any ship cometh in, she taketh first pilots to sound the way, which, in effect, is reputed to be one of the greatest sureties that the Venetians have for defense of their city against all enemies by sea; and then by land it is impossible to hurt or besiege it unless the enemy were able to occupy 150-mile compass with his army.

Of buildings

Next unto the situation, the manner of their building is most to be marveled at. For almost every man that buildeth an house maketh his foundation lower than the water and ere ever he set in hand withal is constrained to make such a strong pale of piles and mud between his building and the water as shall be able to defend his work when (after he hath closed it well) the water and mud that resteth within is cleansed and emptied out. Then causeth he strong piles of timber of a great length to be driven in and thereupon with stone and gravel beginneth his foundation. So that when he hath brought it to the full sea-mark, he reckoneth to have furnished one half of his building; notwithstanding that above water I think no place of all Europe able at this day to compare with that city for number of sumptuous houses, specially for their fronts. For he that will row through the Canale Grande and mark well the fronts of the houses on both sides shall see them more like the doings of princes than private men. And I have been with good reason persuaded that in Venice be above 200 palaces able to lodge any king.

But now to the particular of their notable buildings: The new castle at the mouth of the haven Lido for strength and beauty is one of the rarest things done in these days. The Church of

St. Mark is a very antique thing, furnished with goodly pillars of fine marble to the number of 900 (as they say), besides the floor under foot of small marble stones wrought in knots of divers colors and four fair brazen horses over the front. The Duke's palace is a very sumptuous building and not yet finished. The street called *la Piazza di San Marco* is very fair and large, and the one side is built of hard stone, all uniformly with fair glazen windows, and the street below paved over with brick. St. Mark's steeple is a very high and fair tower of brick, so well built that withinforth an horse may be led up into the belfry. The Rialto is a goodly place in the heart of the city where the merchants twice a day assemble. The schools of St. Roch and St. Mark are two notable things, the fronts whereof are the fairest and costliest that ever I have seen.

Finally, the Arsenale in mine eye exceedeth all the rest. For there they have well near 200 galleys in such an order that upon a very small warning they may be furnished out unto the sea. Besides that, for every day in the year (when they would go to the coast) they should be able to make a new galley, having such a staple of timber (which in the water within the Arsenale hath lien a-seasoning, some twenty year, some forty, some an hundred, and some I wot not how long) that it is a wonder to see it. And every of these galleys hath his covering or house by himself on the dry land so that the long lying unoccupied cannot hurt them. Their masts, cables, sails, anchors, rudders, oars, and every other thing are ready in houses of offices by themselves, that, unseen, it is almost incredible, with such a quantity of artillery, both for sea and land, as made me to wonder, besides the harness and weapons that suffice (as they say) to arm an 100,000 men. Finally, the number of workmen waged for term of life about those exercises is wonderful. For by all that I could learn, their ordinary is never less than 600 working in the Arsenale, be it peace or war. And because they have such a number of boatmen that continually live by gain upon the water within the city, they need not to seek further for mariners to furnish their galleys withal. For it was credibly told me that there are no less than 12,000 boats daily serving in those their channels, and almost no boat rowed but of a sufficient mariner. So that if the Venetians had been men as the Romans were, given as well unto chivalry by land as unto the exercise on the water, no doubt they might many years agone have subdued the world. But sure their power hath been more warily governed than valiantly enlarged. For since Constantinople was gotten by the Turks, their dominion hath decreased, both by reason (as the fame goeth) they rather practice with money to buy and sell countries, peace, and war than to exercise deeds of arms, and for that most Venetians are at these days become better merchants than men of war.

And now methinketh it convenient to speak in this place of the armory that is in an hall of the Duke's palace, called *la Sala del Consiglio dei Dieci,* which surely is a very notable thing.

There be (as they reckon) a thousand coats of plate, part covered with cloth of gold and velvet, with gilt nails so fair that princes might wear them, besides divers other fair harnesses made of late, which are bestowed in so fair an order with their divers kinds of weapons, furnished of the best sort, that a great while looking on could not satisfy me. This hall is divided into divers several portions as the house doth give it, and every portion hath his sort by himself very handsomely.

Finally, for provision of fresh water, it is a wonder to see their number of costly wells made only to receive the rain that falleth from the houses. I call them costly because, first, every well hath his bottom as low as the salt water and must therefore be so surely walled and stopped with sand on the utter side that it defend the salt water from soaking in. And on the inner side it must have his vent to receive the water that falleth from the houses, gravel within to pass through, and, last of all, a fair paving of brick or stone in the bottom, closed about like a cistern to preserve the purged water.

And though they have a great number of those wells and plenty of rain, yet the poor men that dwell in the country do gain yearly above 20,000 crowns by bringing their boats laden with fresh water from the rivers to Venice. Yet all this notwithstanding, you shall many times hear much lamentation among the poor folk for lack of water.

Of the dominion

Besides all those towns and habitations that are in their marshes and on that long bank between them and the sea, as Murano, Mazorbo, Torcello, Malamocco, Chiozza, and others, they have on the mainland the country of Friuli, anciently called *Forum Julii,* the cities of Treviso, Padua, Vicenza, Verona, Brescia, Bergamo, and Crema, with their appurtenances; the most part of the country of Istria; and upon the coasts of Dalmatia (now called Slavonia), they have Zara and Sebenico, in the mouth of the Adriatic Sea the isle of Corfu, and in the Levant Seas, otherwise called *Mare Mediterraneum,* the notable islands of Candia and Cyprus. So that if the ground that they be lords of were in one man's hands, he should be no less worthy to be called a king than most kings that are known at these days. For not long agone Cyprus (a part of this) hath had a king alone. And how and when they got these things, this brief history hereafter following particularly declareth.

Of revenue

As I have been credibly informed by some gentlemen Venetians that have had to do therein, they levy of their subjects little less than four millions of gold by the year, which (after our old reckoning) amounted to the sum of ten hundred thousand pounds sterling—a thing rather to be wondered at than believed, considering they raise it not upon lands but upon customs, after so extreme a sort that it would make any honest heart sorrowful to hear it. For there is not a grain of corn, a spoonful of wine, a corn [2] of salt, egg, bird, beast, fowl, or fish bought or sold that payeth not a certain custom. And in Venice specially, the customer's [3] part in many things is more than the owner's. And if anything be taken by the way uncustomed, be it merchandise or other, never so great or small, it is forfeited. For those customers keep such a sort of prollers [4] to search all things as they come to and fro that I think Cerberus was never so greedy at the gates of hell as they be in the channels about Venice. And though they in searching a boat find no forfeiture, yet will they not depart without drinking money. And many times the meanest laborer or craftsman throughout all their dominion payeth a rate for the poll by the month. Insomuch that a Candiot, my friend (one that had dwelled in Constantinople), sware to me by his faith the Christians lived a great deal better under the Turk than under the Venetians. It is almost incredible what gain the Venetians receive by the usury of the Jews, both privately and in common. For in every city the Jews keep open shops of usury, taking gages of ordinary for fifteen in the hundred by the year, and if at the year's end the gage be not redeemed it is forfeit, or at the least done away to a great disadvantage, by reason whereof the Jews are out of measure wealthy in those parts.

Of dignities and offices

They have a Duke, called after their manner *Doge*, who only (amongst all the rest of the nobility) hath his office immutable for term of life, with a certain yearly provision of 4,000 ducats

[2] Grain.   [3] Tax collector.
[4] The obsolete original of "prowler"; that is, a searcher.

or thereabouts. But that is so appointed unto him for certain ordinary feasts and otherlike charges that his own advantage thereof can be but small. And though in appearance he seemeth of great estate, yet in very deed his power is but small. He keepeth no house, liveth privately, and is in so much servitude that I have heard some of the Venetians themselves call him an honorable slave. For he cannot go a mile out of the town without the Council's license, nor in the town depart extraordinarily out of the palace but privately and secretly. And in his apparel he is prescribed an order, so that in effect he hath no manner of pre-eminence but the bare honor, the gift of a few small offices, and the liberty *di mettere una parte,*[5] which is no more but to propound unto any of the councils his opinion touching the order, reformation, or correction of anything; and that opinion every council is bound to accept into a trial of their sentences by ballot (the manner of which balloting shall hereafter appear); and this privilege to have his only opinion balloted no man hath but he. And whereas many have reported that the Duke in balloting should have two voices, it is nothing so, for in giving his voice he hath but one ballot as all others have.

Next unto the Duke are three called the *Signori Capi* [6] or *Cai,* which outwardly seem inferior to the Duke and yet are of more authority than he. For their power is so absolute that, if there happen cause why, they may arrest the Duke. And all such proclamations as concern the majesty of their commonwealth go forth always under their name: like as we use to say, "In the King's name," so say they, *Da parte dei Signori Cai.* Two of which *Cai,* or one of them with one of the *Avogadori,* have power *di mettere una parte,* such as is before rehearsed of the Duke.

[5] Present a motion.

[6] Chief Lords; the three presidents of the criminal court of appeals (the *quarantia criminale*) sat together in the Signoria in rotation in a two-months' term.

Then have they six counselors of the most worthy among them, who are joined with the Duke to sit in the college for audience of ambassadors and other matters of importance, and these specially are called *la Signoria*.[7] For notwithstanding there be divers joined in the same college with them, as *gli savii della terra ferma* [8] and other mo, yet those six counselors are of most reputation in that place and accordingly go always appareled in scarlet or crimson silks.

Indeed, *la Signoria* is commonly used as the name of their whole majesty, and principally it doth include the Duke with the rest of the chief officers or senators (to the number of three-score) that accompanieth him when in his solemnity he cometh to church or goeth unto any of the ordinary ceremonies abroad in the city.

Now of such as have authority to consult upon matters of importance (as, we should say, the King's Majesty's Privy Council), they have seventeen persons appointed called *il Consiglio dei Dieci*,[9] of which the Duke, the three *Cai*, and the six counselors are part. For matters of conclusion of peace, of war, of state, or of otherlike greatest importance, they have a council called *Pregadi*,[10] into the which entereth the Duke with the *Consiglio dei Dieci* and of the other principal officers to the number of 200 or thereabouts.

For matters of justice there be divers other offices, as *il Consiglio di Quaranta, il Consiglio di Trenta, gl'Avogadori, i*

[7] The lordship; alternatively the *collegio minore*, or senior cabinet.

[8] Council for the mainland, or department heads, five in number. Two other such bodies of ministers combined with it to make up the whole *collegio*, or cabinet, of twenty-six members.

[9] The dreaded Council of Ten, which necessarily counted up to twenty (not seventeen) when the Duke and his councilors joined it in regular meetings. The Ten was a kind of emergency legislature, taking over many functions of the Senate.

[10] The invited or elected; actually the Senate, the normal legislative body, numbering 120. Only members of the *collegio*, or cabinet, could initiate action in the Senate.

Signori di Notte, gl'Auditori vecchi e nuovi,[11] and many mo, which have their degrees and orders so appointed that not one of them will meddle with another's office, being a thing no less fearful unto them than poison. For their principal profession is liberty, and he that should usurp upon another should incontinently be reputed a tyrant, which name of all things they cannot abide. For when a subject of theirs saith, "Sir, you are my lord, you are my master," he taketh it for the greatest villainy [12] of the world.

The *Signor della Sanita* [13] hath the charge to see the city kept clean and the sick provided for. And as for other particular officers that have the oversight of all manner provisions and assize of victuals, it shall suffice to say that there cometh nothing unto their city but it is viewed and an ordinary price appointed unto the seller to the intent the buyer be not deceived.

Of the Great Council

Now it behooveth me to say somewhat of their Great Council, which seemeth to be the whole stay of their commonwealth.

There be about 200 families of name, as Contarini, Morosini, Donati, Badoeri, Foscari, and such others, of which families be well near the number of 2,500 gentlemen. And all they that are of the age of twenty-five and upwards do enter into the Great Council, the order of whose admission into the same is: when a gentleman is grown unto twenty year old, his father or friends do present him unto the *Avogadori,* who taketh his name and, with other names of the same sort, putteth it into a box until the fourth of December, being the day appointed that all they of that age resort unto the Duke, unto whom (besides this box)

[11] *Quarantia* (the forty) was the name of three courts, two being *civile* and one *criminale.* The *Trenta* (thirty) I do not identify. The *Avogadori* and the *Auditori* were investigating magistrates, usually prosecutors but also public defenders. The six Night Commissioners were district police magistrates.

[12] Insult.   [13] Health commissioner.

there is brought another box with so many balls as the names amount unto, of which every fifth ball is gold and all the rest silver. Then taketh the Duke a bill out of one box and a ball out of another, and if the bill meet with a golden ball, then is that gentleman allowed, and if he meet not, then must he abide a better chance the next year or else the age of twenty-five.

This foresaid Great Council may be likened to our Parliament, for unto it many matters of importance are appealed,[14] and that that it doth is unreformable. By it all offices are given and into it entereth the Duke and all the other officers. And finally, there pass so many things through that Great Council (specially offices) that ordinarily every holiday, and many times the working days, the same sitteth from dinner till night, the order being this:

They have an hall very fair and large, in the principal part whereof at the one end sitteth the Duke with certain counselors, and over against him at the other end the *Cai,* and on the sides the *Avogadori* with the other magistrates. Then in the body of the hall there be ten long benches from the one end thereof unto the other, and so made that the gentlemen may sit by two rows on a bench back to back. And so every man being set at what place it shall please him to take at his coming in, the doors are shut, and the chancellor standeth up and readeth the office that is void with the names of them that desire it, and he that in the election hath most ballots (so that they pass the half number) is admitted officer. If there be none that hath more than half the voices, as of a 1,000 to have 501, then is the election put over till another day. This manner of giving their voices by ballot is one of the laudablest things used amongst them, for there is no man can know what another doth.

The boxes are made with an hollow place at the top that a man may put in his hand, and at the end of that place hang

[14] It was not, however, a legislative body, but rather the whole (limited) electorate, choosing most officials from the *Doge* down.

two or three boxes, into which, [if] he will, he may let fall his ballot that no man can perceive him. If there be but two boxes (as commonly it is in election), the one saith yea and the other saith nay. And if there be three boxes (which for the most part happeneth in cases of judgment), the one saith yea, the other saith nay, and the third saith nothing, and they are all well enough known by their divers colors. By this order of balloting they proceed in judgment through all offices, upon all manner of causes, being reputed a sovereign preservation of justice. For oftentimes the judges may grant their voices and, nevertheless, when they come to the hearing of the matter, do as their consciences shall lead them, answering afterwards that they did their best but they could not prevail.

Finally, in the disposing of their offices they use this order: that all offices of pre-eminence, as of the *Signoria,* that are before rehearsed, or the being *Potestate,*[15] captain or governor of any city, castle, town, or country, may be given to none other but unto gentlemen Venetians. All offices that be under commandment, as chancellor, secretaries, and such others, are bestowed amongst their best-known citizens. For though there be many of those offices of commandment very profitable, yet can no gentleman have the benefit thereof, either because they will maintain in their personages a certain majesty with their liberty, or else because they will avoid the inconveniences that may grow of perpetuity. For all manner of gentlemen's offices, from the highest to the lowest (the Duke's dignity only excepted), are removable—some from year to year, some every nine months, some more, some less, for no gentleman may long enjoy one office—so all offices that appertain unto their citizens are durable for term of life without any change.

Amongst all other, this notable order they have, that two gentlemen of one family cannot be in one magistrate or high office together at once. By reason whereof, those gentlemen

[15] Abbreviated to *Podestà.*

that of one name are fewest in number grow a great deal sooner and oftener to authority than they that be of the most, which is thought a wonderful help of their unity and concord. For if many of one name should rule at once, they might happen so to agree that it should be an undoing of their commonwealth.

Of the proctors and treasure

There be certain principal officers which should seem exempted from their commonwealth and be nevertheless heads of the same; that is, to wit, twelve of the principalest, called *Procuratori di San Marco*,[16] out of which number the Duke is alway chosen, and those have their offices for term of life, with a certain stipend of an hundred ducats a year or thereabout. Their charge is: some to govern the revenues and treasure of the commonwealth and some the rents and treasure of St. Mark's Church.

As for the treasure of their commonwealth, I could never find the mean to see it, but I have been credibly informed that it is a great sum of ready money locked up in chests (that no man may come at), which is sometime more and sometime less as their wealth or charges increase. And though their revenue be very great, yet considering the often wars that they have, the great wages that the senators and officers receive, the number of strange captains that they wage for term of life, the number of castles and fortresses that they maintain, fortified with watch and ward, their continual costly buildings, and, finally, the unreasonable charge of their Arsenale and of their galleys abroad, I think they cannot lay up any great sum at the year's end.

The other treasure of St. Mark's Church I have seen; the principal thing whereof is a table on the high altar, plated over with silver, graven and enameled, and set full of precious

[16] Proctors of St. Mark, perhaps best called the lords treasurers.

stones of all sorts. And then in a little strong corner on the south side of the Church are certain plates of gold, much like women's partlets,[17] set full of rich stones, a goodly imperial crown for their Duke, two fair unicorn's horns,[18] and divers other things; the value whereof consisteth only in the precious stones, for the gold that is about them is but small in quantity, but the stones are many in number, excellent great and fair, and almost inestimable of price.

Finally, to return unto the proctors: their reputation is the greatest next the Duke's, and there is none can climb unto that dignity but either he must be so worthy, ancient, and notable a man as few like are to be found amongst them, or else so rich that in time of need he hath before his election relieved the commonwealth with the loan of a notable sum of money. Which second sort of election is also come up of late, since money (as some say) hath entered in more reputation than virtue.

Of laws

Their advocates (as we should say, our men of law) study principally the civil laws [19] and, besides that, the statutes and customs of the city, which are so many that in manner they suffice of themselves. But he that substantially considereth the manner of their proceedings shall plainly see that all matters are determined by the judges' consciences and not by the civil nor yet by their own laws. For in every office there be divers judges, and that part that hath most ballots prevaileth ever, be it in matter of debt, of title of land, upon life and death, or otherwise. And in every trial of theft, murder, or such other, the party himself is never suffered to speak. But there be certain advocates

[17] Ornamental neckbands.
[18] The powdered horn of the unicorn was thought to be an antidote to poison.
[19] Roman law.

76

waged of the common revenue, which with no less study plead in their defense than the *Avogadori* in the contrary. One day the *Avogadori* cometh into the court and layeth against the felon that that either by examination, by torture, or by witness hath been proved, and another day cometh in the advocate and defendeth the felon with the best answer he can devise, so that many times the prisoner tarrieth two, three, and sometime four years ere ever he come unto his trial of life and death.

This order they observe in Venice only. For out of Venice the gentleman Venetian that is *Potestate* of the city, town, or place hath absolute power to judge upon all matters himself alone, howbeit every of them hath a council of learned men to advise him what the law commandeth. Besides that, every five years there be certain inquisitors, called *Sindaci*,[20] sent forth to reform extortions and all other things that they find amiss throughout their whole dominion.

Finally, there is a law in Venice that no gentleman Venetian may speak with any ambassador without license of the *Signoria*, for fear of intelligence or of dangerous practice. And because they fear lest civil sedition might be the destruction of their commonwealth, as of divers other it hath been, therefore they have provided an order that when any two gentlemen happen to fall out, either they do so dissemble it that their malice never appeareth to the world or else they agree within themselves. For if it come to the *Signoria's* knowledge, it cannot be chosen but he that is most faulty receiveth a great rebuke, and many times in those cases divers are banished or sharply punished. As for their other laws, though I were sufficiently expert in them, yet partly for briefness and partly because they are not so much necessary to my purpose, I pass them over. But this is clear: there can be no better order of justice in a commonwealth than theirs if it were duly observed. Howbeit corruption (by the advocates' means) is so crept in amongst the judges that poor

[20] Controllers or inspectors.

men many times can want [21] no delays in the process of their matters.

Of war

I find two forces of war, one by sea, another by land.

By sea the Venetians themselves govern the whole, and by land they are served of strangers, both for general, for captains, and for all other men of war, because their law permitteth not any Venetian to be captain over an army by land, fearing, I think, Caesar's example. Nevertheless, with their army by land they send forth divers of their gentlemen, some as legates, some as paymasters, so that their general (what nobleman soever he be) hath always a council of the Venetians about him, by whom in manner all things are done.

And by sea every galley hath one gentleman Venetian for captain, by the name of *Sopracòmito*,[22] and over a number of galleys one legate (as it were, an admiral) that may hang and punish at his pleasure. This is ordinary both in peace and war. For though the peace be never so sure and quiet, yet fail they not to send forth yearly certain armed galleys to keep the seas against corsales [23] and pirates, not only because their merchandise may pass safely to and fro but also for the honor that they claim in the dominion thereof. For yearly on the Ascension Day, the Duke with the Senate in their best array use to go into the haven at Lido and, by throwing a ring into the water, to take the sea as their spouse.

Finally, when they hap to have any dangerous war by sea or land, they create a *Provveditore*,[24] who (out of Venice) is of no less authority than the dictator was wont to be in Rome,

[21] Lack (or escape).

[22] Chief captain.

[23] A variant of *corsaro,* "corsair" (Latin *cursarius*).

[24] Literally "purveyor"; in practice, a high commissioner or chief commissar.

specially by sea. And lightly they never make a *Provveditore* but either they be in great fear or peril. And throughout all their dominion, within any city or walled town, no man may carry weapon without a special license.

Of common provision and charitable deeds

Their diligent use in provision for grain is notable. For be it dear or good cheap, their common graner (which is a mighty great house) is in manner always furnished. So that lightly in the city can be no great dearth, because many times of their own common purse they are contented to lose for the poor people's relief, though another time they pay themselves the double.

They have also certain schools or fellowships gathered together for devotion, as one of St. Mark, another of St. Roch, one of this saint, another of that, which, being for the most part substantial men, do relieve a number of the poor after this sort.

They give them once a year a coarse livery with a certain small stipend, for the which the poor man is bound to carry a taper at one of the brethren's or sisters' burial and, besides that, to attend certain holidays at the school, where the principal brethren assemble to dispose unto the marriage of poor young women and in other good works that part of money that their rate for the time doth allow, and afterwards with their priests and clerks go a procession a certain circuit, in the which the poor men likewise carry their tapers before them.

Furthermore, there are certain hospitals, some for the sick and diseased and some for poor orphans, in which they are nourished up till they come unto years of service, and then is the man-child put unto a craft and the maidens kept till they be married. If she be fair, she is soon had and little money given with her; if she be foul, they advance her with a better portion of money.

For the plague, there is an house of many lodgings two miles from Venice, called the *Lazaretto*, unto the which all they of that house wherein one hath been infected of the plague are incontinently sent and a lodging sufficient appointed for them till the infection cease that they may return.

Finally, for prisoners they have this order: twice a year, at Christmas and Easter, the *Auditori* [25] do visit all the prisons in Venice and there give audience unto all creditors that have any debtor in prison for the sum of fifty ducats and under. If the party be able to pay, days [26] are given and sureties found, and if the debt be desperate, then do they themselves agree with the party for more or less, as the likelihood is, and pay him of the common purse. So that ere ever they depart they empty the prisons of all them that lie for that sum.

Of customs in their living

To speak of the gentleman Venetian's private life and customs I wot not whether it be best to follow the common report or to dissemble the matter. And yet meseemeth I cannot do more indifferently than recite what is used to be said on both sides.

If any man would say there were no worthy men amongst the Venetians, he should greatly err. For (as I believe) there be some, and specially of those old fatherly men, as wise, as honest, as faithful, as honorable, and as virtuous as in any place can be found; likewise some of the young men as gentle, as liberal, as valiant, as well learned, as full of good qualities as may be. But to speak of the greater number, strangers use to report that the gentleman Venetian is proud, disdainful, covetous, a great niggard, a more lecher, spare of living, tyrant to his tenant, finally never satisfied with hoarding up of money. For though (say they) he have eight, nine, or ten thousand ducats of yearly revenue, yet will he keep no mo persons in his house but his wife and children, with two or three women servants and one man, or two at the most, to row his gondola. He will go to the market himself and spend so miserably that many a mean man

[25] Examining magistrates (of the civil court).   [26] Due dates.

shall fare better than he. Of his 10,000 ducats a year, if he spend three or four hundred in his house he esteemeth it a wonderful charge.[27] Besides all this, he hath two or three Jews that chop and change [28] with him daily, by whose usury he gaineth out of measure. And yet will he rather see a poor man starve than relieve him with a penny. It is true he will have his wife go gay and sumptuously appareled, and on his woman besides, if he be a lover (as in manner they be all), he will stick for no cost. To the marriage of his daughter thirty or forty or fifty thousand ducats is no marvel. Finally, his greatest triumph is when St. Mark hath need (for under that name is comprehended their commonwealth), to be able to disburse an huge sum of money in loan, to receive yearly till he be repaid ten, twelve, or fifteen of the hundred.

This kind of prest [29] the *Signoria* useth to take (borrowing of all them that are able to lend) when they happen to have wars. And they that may do the more willingly lend because they are not only well paid again with the usury but also the more honored and favored as long as their money is out of their hands.

This is their trade,[30] saith the stranger. But the Venetian, to the contrary, defendeth himself on this wise:

"Admit" (saith he) "that this report were true. If I be proud, I have good cause, for I am a prince and no subject. If I be spare of living, it is because my commonwealth alloweth no pomp, and measure is wholesome. If I keep few servants, it is because I need no mo. If I buy my meat myself, it is because I will eat that that I love, and that (having little ado) I will exercise myself withal. As for my tenant, he liveth by me, and I am no tyrant for husbanding mine own. If I gain, I gain

---

[27] Expense. Thomas later counts the ducat as equal to five shillings fourpence, or three and one-fifth ducats to the pound sterling. The 10,000 ducats here in question would be some £3,150, a large income.

[28] Buy and sell (financial transactions).　　　　[29] Loan.

[30] Practice, implying a nation devoted to money-making.

upon my money and hide not my talent in the ground. If I love, I hate not; if she be fair, I am the more worthy. If I spend little, I have the more in my purse. If I spend largely with my daughter, it is because I will bestow her on a gentleman Venetian to increase the nobility of mine own blood and by mean of such alliance to attain more ability to rule and reign in my commonwealth; besides that, my money, if her husband die, is hers and no man's else. If my wife go gay, it is to please mine eye and to satisfy her. In keeping my money to lend unto St. Mark, it is both an help to my commonwealth and a profit unto myself." And thus defendeth the Venetian it that in manner all the world layeth unto his charge.

But surely many of them trade and bring up their children in so much liberty that one is no sooner out of the shell but he is hail fellow with father and friend, and by that time he cometh to twenty years of age, he knoweth as much lewdness as is possible to be imagined. For his greatest exercise is to go amongst his companions to this good woman's [31] house and that, of which in Venice are many thousands of ordinary less than honest. And no marvel of the multitude of their common women, for among the gentlemen is a certain use that if there be divers brethren, lightly but one of them doth marry, because the number of gentlemen should not so increase that at length their commonwealth might wax vile; [32] wherefore the rest of the brethren do keep courtesans to the intent they may have no lawful children. And the bastards that they beget become most commonly monks, friars, or nuns, who by their friends' means are preferred to the offices of most profit, as abbots, priors, and so forth. But specially those courtesans are so rich that in a mask, or at the feast of a marriage, or in the shroving time, you shall see them decked with jewels as they were queens. So that it is thought no one city again able to compare with Venice for the

[31] An obvious euphemism. [32] Poor.

number of gorgeous dames. As for their beauty of face, though they be fair indeed, I will not highly commend them, because there is in manner none, old or young, unpainted. Indeed, of their stature they are for the most part very goodly and big women, well made and strong.

The liberty of strangers

All men, specially strangers, have so much liberty there that though they speak very ill by the Venetians, so they attempt nothing in effect against their state, no man shall control them for it. And in their *Carnevale* time (which we call Shrovetide) you shall see maskers disguise themselves in the Venetians' habit and come unto their own noses in derision of their customs, their habit, and misery.

Further, he that dwelleth in Venice may reckon himself exempt from subjection. For no man there marketh another's doings, or that meddleth with another man's living. If thou be a papist, there shalt thou want no kind of superstition to feed upon. If thou be a gospeler,[33] no man shall ask why thou comest not to church. If thou be a Jew, a Turk, or believest in the devil (so thou spread not thine opinions abroad), thou art free from all controlment. To live married or unmarried, no man shall ask thee why. For eating of flesh in thine own house, what day soever it be, it maketh no matter. And generally of all other things, so thou offend no man privately, no man shall offend thee, which undoubtedly is one principal cause that draweth so many strangers thither.

[33] Evangelical; that is, Protestant.

An Abridgment of the Venetian Histories from the Edification of the City unto This Day

[We omit these chronicles (ff. 83v–110v) until they reach Thomas' own time.]

AFTER Barbarico, Leonardo Loredano was elected to the state, in whose time all Christian princes about the Venetians conspired by one accord utterly to destroy them. And the league was such that in one self time the Emperor Maximilian; Lewis the Twelfth, French king; Ferdinando, King of Spain and of Naples; Julius, Bishop of Rome; with the Dukes of Mantua and Ferrara, should war upon them, beginning about the year of grace 1509. So partly by force, after many discomfitures of the Venetians' power, partly by accord, in manner all the Venetian dominion within the mainland was divided amongst these princes. The French king had Brescia, Bergamo, Cremona, and Crema; the Emperor Maximilian, Verona, Vicenza, Padua, and part of Friuli; the King of Spain, the cities and ports in Puglia that the Venetians before had gotten; the Bishop of Rome, Rimini, Faenza, Ravenna, and Cervia, with the rest of Romagna; and the Duke of Ferrara, the Polisene di Rovigo. So that the Venetians had so little dominion left on the mainland that the Emperor Maximilian came to Mestre, five little miles from Venice, as near as the sea would suffer him to approach, and there, for a triumph or despite, shot off his artillery to Venicewards, though he could do it no hurt. Wherefore the Venetians, provoked in manner by despair and through an oration made by their Duke that encouraged them rather to die like men than to suffer themselves thus vilely to be eaten up

84

and despised, renewed an army by land, recovered Padua, then negligently kept, fortified it and Treviso, fought divers times with variable fortune against their enemies, sought to be revenged on the Duke of Ferrara, against whom they sent 17 galleys and 400 boats to assail the Ferrarese dominion by the river of Po, and, finally, behaved themselves so manfully that the King of Spain and the Bishop of Rome made a new league with them against the French king; who at that time, besides the state of Milan, had gotten Bologna and was become so great in Italy that they were all afeard of him. Upon conclusion of which league, the citizens of Brescia returned to the Venetian obedience, so that for defense of that city against the Frenchmen, Andrea Gritti, with certain other noble Venetians and captains and a convenient number of soldiers, were sent thither; where after a sore conflict with the Frenchmen, they were all discomfited, slain, or taken, and the principal prisoners sent to Milan to Monsieur de Foix, then governor there, who sent Andrea Gritti, as a singular present, prisoner to the French king.

The Venetians, not a little troubled for this loss, caused the camp of the league that then lay before Bologna to draw towards Ferrara, and in succor of that camp made a new army by water wherewith they sacked Argenta, took Mirandola, and did much hurt to the Ferrarese dominion, till at last the Viceroy of Spain, general of the said camp, came before Bologna and from thence to Ravenna, for fear of the French host that from Milan pursued him. Unto which French army the Duke of Ferrara united his power and so together followed the army of the league to Ravenna, where on Easter Day [1] in the morning was fought the bloodiest battle between them that hath been heard of in our days, and so many thousands slain on both sides that it could scarcely be judged who had the better, saving that the Frenchmen obtained the victory, took Ravenna, put it to sack, and after gat divers other towns in Romagna.

[1] In 1512.

Whilst these things were doing, the Dutchmen's hall [2] in Venice, called *il Fondaco di Tedeschi*, was re-edified, a very fair and great house and of a marvelous rent. For they affirm that it yieldeth to the Venetians above 100 ducats a day, which after our old reckoning amounteth above 7,000 pound sterling by the year.

After Loredano succeeded Antonio Grimani,[3] who, being in exile, was called home, made proctor of St. Mark, and, finally, Duke.

Then Andrea Gritti, before named, newly returned out of France, was elected Duke; [4] by whose means the Venetians entered in league with the French king and so recovered Brescia, redeemed Verona for a great sum of money, and aided the Frenchmen to recover Milan and to do many feats in the realm of Naples; howbeit the Frenchmen not long after lost all again through their ill governance and tyranny.

Finally, practicing [5] now with France, now with the Emperor, now with the Bishop of Rome, as best served for the commonwealth, this Duke left it in good order, tranquillity, and peace, and so died, greatly bewailed of his citizens.

Then followed Peter Lando,[6] in whose days the Turk made war to the Venetians because they joined with the Emperor against him, so that they to obtain peace were fain to give him the strong and notable cities Nauplia and Malvagia [7] in Greece and, beside that, the sum of 300,000 ducats.

It was thought that the Turk would have been appeased with a much less gift, but, being secretly advertised by the French ambassador how the Venetians had given their Bailo or ambassador commission that, rather than the war should continue, to

---

[2] The house of the German merchants; a combined residence, office, and warehouse.

[3] In 1521.   [4] *Doge*, 1523–1538.   [5] By alliances and "deals."

[6] *Doge*, 1538–1545.

[7] Monemvasia (whence malmsey wine came). Both cities are Aegean ports in the Morea or Peloponnesus.

make this offer, he would none otherwise agree with them.

This knowledge came through intelligence that the French ambassador had with one of the Venetian secretaries, who, through corruption of money, disclosed all the proceedings of the Privy Council; which at length being discovered, the same secretary fled into France and two other Venetians of his confederacy were taken and hanged.

By this man's time, Andrea Doria,[8] with a great navy of the Emperor's, of the Bishop of Rome's, and of the Venetians' together, enterprised a journey against Barbarossa, Admiral of the Turkish navy, and yet meeting with him at great advantage, both of power and place, Doria retired, for what cause no man can tell. He left the Venetian galleon, the notablest vessel of the world, in the midst of the Turk's navy. And yet after she had been assailed five hours on all sides, she came her ways safe in despite of them all, leaving an infinite number of her shot in the Turkish beaten ships and galleys.

After Lando, Francesco Donato was elected unto the state about two years and a half before the writing hereof.[9] And because in his time hitherto hath not happened any worthy thing to the Venetians, I will refer the rest to them that hereafter shall find occasion to write.

The Description of Naples

THE city of Naples (sometime called Parthenope) is one of the fairest cities of the world for goodly streets and beautiful build-

---

[8] The great Genoese admiral. This indecisive campaign, which Thomas has mentioned before as an injury to the Venetian state, took place in 1538.

[9] In 1545.

ing of temples and houses, specially the Castel Nuovo, wherein the kings were wont (as the *Vicerè* now is) to be most commonly resident, being one of the rarest buildings for greatness and strength that anywhere is lightly to be found.

The country about is so pleasant that in manner every village deserveth to be spoken of, as well for sumptuous buildings and number of commodities, namely, abundance of delicate fruits, as also for the wholesome air. For in most places it seemeth always (yea, at the deadest of the winter) to be continual springtime. Indeed, the heat of summer doth somewhat grieve them, but they are so provided of large and open buildings that it doth not much annoy them.

And one thing amongst all the rest is to be marveled at, whereof it should proceed that many times the fire breaketh out of the earth in divers places upon the seacoasts, like to the flames of Mongibello, anciently called *Etna* in Sicily, as in the first year of the Emperor Titus it happened beside Naples in the hill Vesuvio, now called *Somma*, where Pliny the same time (seeking the cause thereof) ended his life, not by violence of the fire (for he approached not so near) but by the vehement oppilation [1] of the sulphur that stopped his breath. It is true that the natural hot bains (whereof there be many in Italy and, namely, in the realm of Naples) come of the natural heat that is in the sulphur, through the veins whereof the water maketh his course, but what should be cause of this flame that (as it were against nature) ascendeth out of the cold earth, almost no man can make any reason. Indeed, the best opinion that I gather is that the vein of sulphur in the earth, receiving sometimes through the extreme heat of the sun a certain kind of fire, kindleth, and as the vein is great or small so worketh it the effect. If it be near the upper part of the earth and have vent, it breaketh out in fire or smoke; if it be so deep that for the great weight of the earth it cannot issue, then doth it cause the earth

[1] Obstructive action.

to quake, as in those parties (most subject to the sun) earthquakes are common, and sometime whole towns and countries are destroyed withal.

Some think the fertility of the realm should proceed much of the heat that this sulphur giveth the ground (seeing there is more plenty than elsewhere), but whereofsoever it cometh, the country is surely replenished of all things necessary for man's life, and so pleasant withal that Pandolfo Collenuccio (a notable writer of the Neapolitan histories) thinketh the wonderful mutations that have happened in the same to proceed of the desire that men had unto the pleasures and commodities of the country. And further speaking of the inconstancy of the people, he saith these words: "It seemeth that the realm of Naples is predestinate to have in it continual tyrannies, seditions, falsehood, rebellions, wars, destruction of cities, ravishments, and flame, with all the other calamities that of avarice and ambition (true mothers of such plagues) may grow"; and alleging the authority of divers ancient writers, affirmeth that the provinces of the realm, which he calleth *regnicoli*, do persevere without rebellion as long as they find none to rebel against. Nevertheless, Titus Livius and the ancient Roman histories show that Naples itself was of all other cities most constant in their faith towards the Romans, as well in time of danger as of prosperity. And for the space of these thirty years and more they have persevered in quiet obedience under their princes. Nevertheless, in this the abridgment of their histories, ye shall see that since the decay of the Roman Empire no realm in all the world hath been so much subject to alterations and wars, principally through occasion of the inhabitants themselves, who always were divided in partakings to their own confusion. And you shall yet to this hour see that the Neapolitans are scarcely trusted on their words. Not that I think they deserve less credit than other men but because the wonted general ill opinion of their unsteadfastness is not taken out of men's hearts. Yet is the Neapolitan for his good entertainment reckoned to be the very courtesy of the world, though most men repute him to be a great flatterer and full of craft. What will you more? They are rich, for almost every gentleman is lord and king within himself; they have very fair women and the world at will, insomuch as Naples contendeth with Venice whether should be preferred for sumptuous dames. Finally, the court about the *Vicerè* was wont to be very princely and greater than that of Milan for train of gentlemen, but now it is somewhat diminished, as you shall perceive in the end of this history.

The saying (of them that best can guess) is that it yieldeth the Emperor three millions of gold by the year, which after our reckoning is about £700,000. A great part whereof is consumed in maintaining the *Vicerè's* state and keeping of many fortresses and in the wages of 300 men of arms continually maintained there, that must keep every one his three horse, for the which he hath as good as fifty pound stipend yearly and many of them have more. And one great fault there is, for almost no stranger can travel the realm unrobbed, specially between Rome and Naples. It is in manner closed about with the sea, except 150 mile that is cut over from the mouth of the river of Ofanto, now called *Maseno,* unto the mouth of Tronto,[2] and is of compass in all, measuring it by the bank, about 1,400 miles, having upon the seacoasts such a number of havens and good towns as few realms christened have the like.

[2] The Ofanto reaches the Adriatic north of Barletta; the Tronto north of Ascoli, the northern boundary of the kingdom. I do not identify Maseno. Ofanto is in fact the modern name of the classical Aufidus.

The History of Naples

[We omit the chronicle of the Kings of Naples since Charlemagne (ff. 114v–135v) until the end of the fifteenth century.]

FINALLY Frederick, brother to the late Alfonso, succeeded to the crown,[1] but ere he had fully reigned four years, hearing of the French king's coming, Lewis the Twelfth, and considering himself destitute of money, friendship, and ability to resist, he sold his armor and munition for 30,000 ducats to the Duke Valentino Borgia, son to the Bishop of Rome, and with the rest of his treasure and implements went into France and there yielded both himself and his realm into the French king's hands, who received him and, appointing him an honorable provision, kept him in France till he died. And thus ended the reign of the house of Aragon in the realm of Naples.

And though upon the surrender of this Frederick (whom many charge with cowardice for the vile submitting of himself without any proof of force) the French king obtained the whole realm, yet he died, not long enjoying it, either by reason of the intolerable proud behavior of the French governors or else through the inconstant nature of the Neapolitans; Ferdinando, King of Spain (commonly called *Il Re Catholico*), comforted thereunto by many of the barons and specially by the citizens of Naples, sent a puissant army into the realm against the Frenchmen; who within less than two years, partly by force and partly by treaty, were clean expulsed, so that in fine the realm rested wholly in peaceable possession of the Spanish king.[2]

---

[1] In 1496.   [2] In 1502.

Ferdinando, the fifth of that name, King of Spain, chasing away the Frenchmen, enjoyed quietly the realm of Naples unto his death and easily recovered of the Venetians the four ports in Puglia that Ferrandino had given them. By reason that when all the Christian princes were entered into a league at Cambrai against the Venetians, they at that time made none offer of resistance but rather consented unto the rendering of them, like as in hope of peace they granted unto all the other princes what they would ask, Venice only excepted.

Finally, Ferdinando deceasing, Charles the Fifth, now Emperor of Almain (son and heir of Philip, Duke of Burgundy, and of Joan his wife, eldest daughter and heir of the forenamed King Ferdinando), succeeded in the realm of Naples,[3] as he did in all the other realms and dominions that Ferdinando had, and hitherto enjoyeth the same.

It is true that the French king sent Monsieur de Lautrec, his general, with a puissant army to conquer the realm, where between the parties French and Spanish were done many worthy deeds of arms. Naples itself was besieged by sea and land until Andrea Doria, general of the French king's army by sea, revolted from the French king to the service of the Emperor, from which time the hope of the French army's prosperity began to abate and fortune so much to go against them that—what through extreme plague and through the hardiness of the imperials that began to take courage—the Frenchmen were constrained to raise their siege, Monsieur de Lautrec, with many other of the best French captains, being dead, some of the plague and some of the sword, so that of 60,000 which under the French standard came thither to the siege escaped not fully 2,000 on live.[4] From which time hitherwards the Emperor hath had no notable trouble there, saving that now of late is begun a little strife between the *Vicerè* Don Diego di Toledo and the barons of the realm for making of certain laws, and some bicker-

[3] In 1516.   [4] In 1528.

ing and slaughter hath happened between the Spaniards and them, and many gentlemen are fled to Rome and other places for fear of punishment. But because the thing is not of such importance as should seem to move war, I shall not need to make further rehearsal.

The Description of Florence

FLORENCE, an excellent fair city, standeth at the foot of the Apennine Hills in a little valley, named *Arno,* of the river Arno that runneth through it. Coming to it (excepted by the riverside), the descending is such that a man may easily behold every part of the city, without the which, down along both sides of the valley, are so many fair palaces and sumptuous houses that for the space of eight or ten miles it seemeth in manner but one town.

The city itself is esteemed to be seven miles in compass, walled with square stone in manner as hard as flint and of a great height, with a number of goodly towers after the ancient building, strong enough to defend but nothing apt for artillery to offend after the manner of these days, for they were builded before the invention of guns.[1]

Over the river within the city are four very fair bridges of square stone; on the furthest down the river hath been a little marble image of Mars, which was set there by an astronomer about the first building of the city in such a conjunction of the celestial bodies that it promised prosperity to the city as long as that image should stand, threatening the decay of the

[1] Thomas evidently does not include the modern walls on the hills south of the Arno, which Michelangelo helped to build before the siege of 1530.

same as soon as it were gone. And as I have been credibly informed, within less than these twenty years it fell and is gone, no man can tell how. Shortly whereupon the Emperor's army besieged the Florentines and took their liberty from them.

The river Arno is not lightly big, but once a year, when the sun hath power to dissolve the snow on the mountains, it swelleth so that it may in manner be compared to Thames at London, saving it serveth not for vessel to come from the sea by reason of the swift stream. Wherefore the Florentines are fain for the most part to fetch their merchandise that come by sea from Pisa, forty miles off by land.

Within the city are many goodly temples and other edifices, amongst the which the cathedral church is an excellent fair building. For the walls without are all covered with fine white and black marble, wonderfully well wrought, and over the choir is an whole vault called cupola, fashioned like the half of an egg, rising between three aisles and the body of the church, so artificially made that almost it seemeth a miracle. For it is so high that the pommel on the top, being able to contain seven persons, seemeth a very small thing to them that stand below. And the compass of it by the base is about 160 paces. Besides that, the floor under this vault round about the choir is laid with fine marble of divers colors so fair that it yieldeth a delight to them that walk upon it.

The steeple [2] standing beside the church is likewise of fine marble, a very fair and square tower, equal in height to the circuit of the base, with divers stories and things graven in it, so artificial and costly that it deserveth singular praise.

The Temple of St. John, called *Il Battesimo*, is likewise of fine marble both within and without, having a number of goodly pillars and three brazen gates very sumptuous and fair. Many other goodly churches there be which should be too long here to rehearse.

[2] The campanile of Giotto.

Description of Florence

The Duke's palace,[3] with the place before it, representeth a very stately and ancient majesty. On the backside thereof is the house wherein the wild beasts are kept, as lions, tigers, bears, wolves, apes, eagles, gripes,[4] and such other, whereof there be not a few.

The two principal houses of Strozzi and Medici seem rather the buildings of princes than of private men. And generally the citizens' houses for their beauty are worthy of much praise. Howbeit they may make them good cheap because they have marble and stone plenty in the mountains thereby, insomuch that all their streets, which are very fair, large, and straight, are paved with flat stone. But amongst all other they have divers goodly hospitals for relief of the sick and poor, and one very fair,[5] so well ordered that it receiveth a great number of men and women, but into several houses, where they are applied with good physic, and their beds, their sheets, and every other thing so clean that many times right honest men and women be not ashamed to seek their health there. For that hospital alone may dispend yearly above 20,000 crowns, by reason whereof they have excellent physicians, good apothecaries, diligent ministers, and every other thing necessary.

Finally, there is a very fair and strong castle called *Cittadella*, more than a mile and [a] half in compass, builded by the last Duke Alexander for a bridle to the Florentines because he had then newly taken their liberties from them, they being for the most part so variable and inconstant that the other Italians have used to call them *bizzarri*, which signifieth wild-headed.

Three miles without the city the Duke hath made a garden at a little house that was his father's.[6] Wherein is a labyrinth or maze of box full of cypress trees, having in the midst one the fairest conduit of white marble that ever I saw; besides

[3] The Palazzo Vecchio, which Cosimo occupied from 1540 to 1550.
[4] Originally griffins, but presumably here meaning vultures (*grifo*).
[5] Santa Maria Nuova.   [6] The Villa di Castello.

that it hath divers other conduits and such conveyances that in manner every flower is served with running water, and all the channels are of white marble, so fair that it is in my judgment at this present one of the excellentest things in all Europe.

The Florentines' customs

The common opinion is that the Florentines are commonly great talkers, covetous, and spare of living, but they be fine and cleanly.

Indeed, he that buyeth at the shambles more meat than their manner there alloweth is incontinently noted and spoken of. But for all the lack that is laid to them as a reproach, yet did I never see it so scarce that a reasonable man ought to find fault withal. And if men generally in other places could follow it, the rich should live more healthfully and the poor find more plenty.

I continued there a certain space at mine own charges and lay a good while with Master Bartholomew Panciatico, one of the notablest citizens, where I never saw the fare so slender but any honest gentleman would have been right well contented withal. And yet I dare avow he exceeded not the ordinary. Besides that, the fine service, the sweetness of the houses, the good order of all things, and the familiar conversation of those men were enough to feed a man, if without meat men might be fed. I will not deny but many of them use much talk, which I think proceedeth of the desire they have to seem eloquent. For he is not reputed a man among them that cannot play the orator in his tale, as well in gesture as in word. And therefore I suppose their Academy was first ordained, which is one of the goodliest orders that I have seen.

A certain number of the chief of them, being well learned, are drawn into a company, whereof the Duke himself is one. These every holiday at three of the clock at afternoon assemble in an hall appointed, where one of them mounteth into a place called the "harange," [7] a little higher than the rest, and in his own mother tongue maketh an oration of an hour long of what matter soever he thinketh best himself. This orator hath warning so to do by an officer a great space before his day. For they choose every half year a Consul, who appointeth a sundry man to the harange for every holiday. And when the hour of assembly approacheth, the most part of the company repair to the Consul and so bring him honorably to the place, where he sitteth highest though the Duke himself be present. And for my part, I never heard reader in school nor preacher in pulpit handle themselves better than I have heard some of these in the harange.

The Florentines' wives are nothing so gay as the Venetians'. For they love a modesty in their women's apparel and, specially if she pass the age of forty, lightly she weareth but plain black cloth. And they keep their maidens so strait that in manner no stranger may see them.

The common people are very religious and for the most part full of superstition, but they that are reckoned wisest believe much with Pliny. And where they have been much burdened with sodomy in time past, I cannot perceive there is any such thing now.

Of the Duke's dominion and revenue

Besides Florence, the Duke hath under his dominion six cities, Pisa, Volterra, Pistoia, Arezzo, Cortona, and Borgo,[8] with divers other good towns and the greatest part of Tuscany, and may dispend better than 500,000 crowns of yearly revenue, the greatest part whereof riseth upon the ten [per cent] that is paid him of all the lands within his dominion.

[7] Medieval Latin *harenga*, giving in Italian *arringa*, "harangue," and *arringo*, "harangue" or "pulpit."
[8] Borgo San Sepolcro, now San Sepolcro.

Of the Edification and Success of the City of Florence

CONFERRING the discourse of divers authors together touching the Florentine histories and finding the effects of them all gathered in one by Niccolò Machiavelli, a notable learned man and secretary of late days to the commonwealth there, I determined to take him for mine only author in that behalf.

It is manifest that from the ancient city of Fiesole (the old ruins whereof are yet to be seen on the top of an hill two miles from Florence) the city of Florence had her beginning principally. For by reason Fiesole stood high and was painful for merchantmen to bring their carriage unto, the citizens kept their market on the side of the river Arno in the plain where Florence now standeth, and building there shops for their wares, from shops they grew to houses and from a few to many, so that at length it became a town, which increased much through certain colonies of the Romans, sent thither first by Sulla and after by those three Romans which after the death of Caesar divided the Empire between them.

And albeit that some have contended upon the name, affirming that it was first called *Fluentia* and after corrupted *Florentia*, yet mine opinion, agreeing with Machiavelli, is that from the beginning it was called *Florentia*. Under the Roman Empire and about the beginning of the Emperors it seemeth to take first name and reputation.

[We omit the medieval history of Florence (ff. 140v–155) and resume with the death of Lorenzo de' Medici in 1492. Machiavelli's history stops here, by the way.]

Edification of Florence

Finally, the most renowned private man of his time, Laurence de' Medici, died, leaving one of his sons a cardinal (who was called thereunto being not fully thirteen years old), and his eldest son Peter in great reputation, and his daughters also very well married.

He favored cunning men, specially them that were learned; he was eloquent in reasoning, quick of invention, wise in determining, and hardy in doing. Besides the conspiracy brought against him when his brother was slain, he was twice in peril of death by treason and yet prevented them both, to the confusion of the conspirators. All the princes of Italy honored him, the King Matthew of Hungary showed him great signs of love, the Soldan of Egypt sent him presents and ambassadors, the Turk delivered Bernardo Bandini, that slew his brother Julian, into his hands, and his own citizens so much loved him that I think of his time died no man happier than he. Contrariwise, his son Peter de' Medici, who, notwithstanding his gentle entertainment of all men at the beginning (which made the world to hope well of him), did at length prove so ambitious, so willful, and so undiscreet in his proceedings that neither the magistrates, the citizens, nor yet the people could well bear him; to the increase whereof, when Charles the Eighth, French king, passed by Florence towards Naples, Peter met him on the way and said to him that his father commanded him three things: the first, to honor God; the second, to worship the French king; and the third, to defend his country. So that Charles, seeing him thus well disposed, entreated him so fair that he delivered into his hands Sarzana, Pietrasanta, and, finally, set Pisa at liberty; which was so great a hindrance to the Florentine state that the magistrates and commons, moved of just disdain, drave him out of the city,[1] took his goods and patrimony as forfeit, and condemned him to perpetual exile with a number of his friends and partakers; and the fury of the people

---

[1] In 1494.

was such that they brake and defaced all the arms that could be found of the Medicis in Florence.

And albeit that he attempted many ways to recover his country, yet was his fortune so ill that the more he stirred the more was he hated; which at length was the undoing both of himself and of a great many mo, as well of his adherents as of his adversaries.

Thus the family of Medici lost reputation and credit for the time, so that the state of Florence returned unto the common rule of the magistrates and citizens; that endured till the time that Leo the Tenth, of the family of Medici, was made Bishop of Rome, who, though he restored not his house unto the full rule they had before in the city, did nevertheless so much, partly with authority and partly by friendship, that divers of that name were received and made partakers of the commonwealth; which by little and little so increased again that in the time of Bishop Clement the Seventh, who also was of the Medici, when the Duke of Bourbon passed by Florence to Romewards,[2] the commons of the city made a commotion against Hippolito de' Medici, then governor of the same, he then being departed out of the city in company of the Cardinal of Cortona to go visit the Duke of Urbino. But as soon as he returned he did so much that they yielded themselves again unto him upon covenant he should hurt no man for that matter.

Then Bishop Clement made this Hippolito a cardinal, whereupon he left the administration of the commonwealth, and so was the city at liberty again. But Clement, being determined to make it perpetual subject to his own family, handled himself so well towards the Emperor at his coronation at Bologna that he obtained the imperial power to the oppression of his own natural country and brought to pass that the Prince of Orange with the Emperor's army besieged Florence.

[2] In 1527, before the sack of Rome.

This siege endured a whole year; which, for the many enterprises and battles fought on both parts, may be compared to the best Trojan, Greekish, or Roman wars, namely because the commonwealth alone, without help of any other prince or state, sustained the violence of two so mighty powers as the Emperor's and the Bishop's of Rome until famine, and not force, overcame them.

Finally, the Prince of Orange and divers other notable captains being slain in the often battles and skirmishes, at last the Florentines for lack of victuals were fain to fall to composition and yielded upon these conditions: [3] that the city should continue in her liberty, referring the reformation of the state to the Emperor, who within the term of four months should thereupon declare his pleasure; that all banished men should be reconciled without remembrance of any injury before passed; that the Medici should be restored to their goods taken from them by violence of the magistrates; that the city should pay 80,000 crowns to the dispatch of the army; with other covenants of less moment. Upon which accord Bartholomew Valori, commissary for the Bishop of Rome, entered with divers of the imperial captains and there behaved themselves so stoutly that (notwithstanding the covenants of peace) they found the mean within less than a month to behead six of the chiefest citizens and to confine 150, besides a number of others that abandoned and fled the city of themselves, so that their promised liberty was turned into a most cruel servitude.

Shortly after came Alexander de' Medici, nephew to Bishop Clement, sent by the Emperor out of Flanders; who at his first coming made a show of sobriety in going privately unto his house and receiving the citizens amiably, but yet at length by little and little he usurped the offices and magistrates and finally disposed them all at his pleasure, causing himself openly to be called Duke.

[3] In August, 1530.

Then died Clement the Bishop, whereupon the Cardinals de' Medici and Salviati, with the principal of the other banished Florentines (coveting the recovery of their city's liberty), sent ambassadors to the Emperor, beseeching him to consider the tyranny of Duke Alexander (who then newly had builded the Cittadella) and to regard the conditions of peace. Which ambassadors arrived at Barcelona even as the Emperor was taking ship towards the enterprise of Tunis; [4] so that, being returned to Rome, the Cardinal Hippolito de' Medici disposed himself to go unto Tunis therefor and, taking his journey towards Naples, died at Itri by the way, poisoned (as the voice went) by procurement of Duke Alexander.

This Duke Alexander was yet but young, who by Bishop Clement's procurement had married the Emperor's bastard daughter; he was so stout that without any respect he would have his will in all things, and, namely, in feats of love and change of women was his special delight. And amongst all other he delighted more in the company of Laurence de' Medici (that should succeed him in the state) than of any other man. But Laurence, instead of that love, hated the Duke, and had long time determined to slay him when he might find occasion —whether he did it in hope the rather to attain to the dominion himself or to restore to the city her ancient liberty be divers opinions.

In effect, without making any man privy to his intent other than a servant of his own, the Duke being on a night all alone in Laurence's house and sleeping on a bed, Laurence and his man slew him; [5] and thereupon counseling with certain of his friends and seeing no man disposed to stand with him in pursuing of his purpose, the selfsame night he fled and went straight to Venice, where in company of the Strozzi he lived, till of late

[4] In 1535.

[5] On January 5, 1537. The assassin was Lorenzino, or Lorenzaccio, as he was later to be called, as in De Musset's play of that name.

certain persons in hope of the *taglia* (a reward proclaimed for the killing of notable offenders) he was also slain.

Immediately upon knowledge of the death of Duke Alexander, the three Florentine cardinals that were then in Rome departed thence and, making all the men they could by the way, came with an army to Florence. Wherefore the Medici, with their friends in Florence (to make their party good that the banished men should not prevail to their destruction), elected Cosimo de' Medici to be their duke, a young man of twenty years of age, whose father John de' Medici had been a man right valiant in arms.[6] And thereupon sent to the cardinals, praying them to stay their army by the way and to come themselves privately to Florence where they should find so much reason offered them that they should need to use no force. So they stayed their power beside Cortona and, being come to Florence, were entreated with so fair promises that they licensed their men to depart. By reason whereof the Duke that now is, with his friends, had time to make themselves strong and then would consent to nothing that the cardinals looked for; so that with a plain mock they departed, lamenting their folly that they had changed the surety of their force for the unsurety of fair words.

This change in Florence and the mock that the cardinals received so much increased their malice that they, with the help of Philip Strozzi and Bartholomew Valori, assembled and waged the number of 4,000 men, which by Peter Strozzi (that yet liveth and serveth the French king) should have been conducted to Montemurlo and from thence to Florence had not Philip and Bartholomew (who with a small company came before to Montemurlo) been set upon by Alexander Vitelli, taken, and led away prisoners to Florence, where the whole conspiracy of those confederates that were in the town was discovered and divers taken and put to execution, and so the

[6] The famous soldier Giovanni delle Bande Nere.

whole enterprise broken and destroyed. Amongst the rest, only Philip Strozzi was preserved from death, notwithstanding he was kept in prison in the Cittadella and there died. Some say he killed himself rather than he would undo his children by paying the ransom that was required of him, being indeed one of the richest private men that was in his time, as it doth well appear by the wealth of his son Peter and of his other children; which, being banished men and having nothing in their own country, do nevertheless live abroad in so much reputation that few brethren of Christendom under the degree of princes do the like.

I have spoken before of Cittadella, builded by Duke Alexander for the more surety of his dominion, which at his death remained in the keeping of one of the Duke's captains. But as soon as Alexander Vitelli (one that had served well the Emperor in his wars) heard of the Duke's death, he came to Florence and entered into the castle to speak with the captain; where he handled the matter so well that he excluded the captain and kept it himself. And though he made many fair promises to Duke Cosimo, yet at length he delivered it to the Emperor, who therefore rewarded him with fair possessions in the realm of Naples.

This Duke Cosimo sued first to marry with the wife of Duke Alexander, the Emperor's daughter, but the Bishop of Rome that now is purchased her (to his no small cost) for his son's son, Duke Ottavio. For the which there hath been mortal hate between Duke Cosimo and the Bishop. And being thus prevented, the Duke, to obtain the more stay towards the Emperor, married [7] the daughter of Don Diego de Toledo, *Vicerè* of Naples, by whose mean he hath redeemed the Cittadella of the Emperor for the sum of 400,000 ducats and is now absolute lord and king within himself.

[7] In 1539. Cosimo secured an imperial patent sanctioning his use of the title Duke of Florence. In 1569 he was created Grand Duke of Tuscany.

He hath divers fair children by his wife and loveth her so well that in manner he never goeth abroad (unless it be to church) without her and is reputed to be a very chaste man. He is learned and wise; he useth few words and is nevertheless in his own tongue eloquent. In the administration of justice he is so sincere that since the time of his reign, which is now above ten years, I have not heard that he hath pardoned any person condemned to die. He hath restrained the vice of sodomy (which heretofore reigned more in Florence than elsewhere in Italy) with pain of death and hath brought his state to such quietness as it hath not been this 300 years past; so that Florence may well say that in him she hath found her long-desired liberty.[8] For though he absolutely hath the whole revenues to his own use, yet the surety that the Florentines have in their own things (which heretofore they never had) is much more worth to them than the common revenue was beneficial to the city.

Finally, the virtue of this Duke Cosimo, besides the worthiness of his dominion, hath brought him in such reputation that he is now numbered as one of the rarest princes of our time and feared also as one in whom there be hid things of greater moment than the rule of that only state.

The State of Genoa

GENOA standeth in manner between the Alps and Apennine Hills and hath his prospect toward the south. For it hangeth so on the descent of the hill that being in the sea underneath a man may almost discern every part of the city. It hath no plain country near it but on the one side hills and mountains and the

---

[8] In the sense of national independence, as well as ruthless law and order at home.

sea Mediterraneum on the other. And yet those hills that run along the seacoasts bring forth many kinds of pleasant fruit, with much wine and oil, for the most part not through fertility of the ground but through the inhabitants' painful diligence.

The circuit of Genoa is little less than five miles; the walls about are very new, fair, and strong, specially, the two gates di San Tommaso and dell' Arco are so large that they seem almost two fortresses.

The haven that cometh into it is exceeding fair and big enough to receive any navy, being forced somewhat narrow at the mouth with a wonderful costly pier of stone made out into the sea; at the end whereof is a strong tower called *Il Molo*, whereby the haven is defended from all winds, the southwest excepted. Within this haven they have an arsenal, able to receive eighteen or twenty galleys.

Their churches are very fair and sumptuous, specially the Cathedral Church of St. Laurence, whose front of white and black marble seemeth a very rare piece of work.

Their houses are exceeding fair, the fronts two stories high, for the most part of fine marble curiously wrought. For their law alloweth none to deck his house any higher with that kind of work (unless it be in respect of some notable service), because it would require an infinite charge to garnish them of that sort to the top, their houses being for the most part six, seven, and some eight stories high. And yet are they so fair that I wot not unto what city I may compare their buildings. And not only within the city but all along the seacoasts, called *la Riviera*, every village is so furnished with gallant and sumptuous houses that it is a world to behold.

Amongst all other the palace of Andrea Doria, without the gate of St. Thomas, is a notable thing, very fair, sumptuous, and large. And above his house (a thing wonderful) he hath made his slaves to hew out of the hard rocky mountain as much space as hath made six gardens, one above another, and hath caused so much earth to be carried up as sufficeth for the growth of all manner fruits and herbs, very pleasant to behold. Likewise, within the town, Andrea Doria hath the goodliest house that any private man hath builded in our days.

But the streets of the city for the most part are so narrow that it is a great defacing to the rest, which I think the steep descent of the hill causeth, that they have not room enough to make their streets large.

Half a mile without the town westwards they have a very fair watchtower called *Torre della Luminaria,* wherein nightly burneth a great light for a mark to them that be on the sea, because it may be discerned very far off.

Finally, they have a very fair conduit of water conveyed on arches, much after the ancient Roman fashion, for the space of five miles or more out of the valley of Bisagno, notwithstanding that they have divers fair springs and one specially that cannot be drawn dry.

Of their dominion and governance

Their dominion is not very great; it passeth not the bounds of Liguria, which is scarcely eighty miles in length and nothing so much in breadth, and may dispend in public revenue not fully 400,000 crowns by the year,[1] as I have been informed. Indeed, in time past they had much greater dominion, so that the common rent [2] hath been very great, but the Turks' prosperity hath much abated that. Nevertheless, it is thought the private citizens were never more wealthy than they be at this present.

Of their trade and customs

All the Genoese in manner are merchantmen and very great travelers of strange countries. For I have been reasonably persuaded that there be five or six thousand of them continually abroad, either merchants or factors, so that they leave few

[1] Twice that of the King of England (see note 29, p. 14 above).
[2] Public revenue.

107

places of the world unsought where any gain is to be had. For the merchandise that they bring home hath speedy dispatch, by reason their city is as a key unto all the trade of Lombardy and to a great part of Italy. They at home make such a number of silks and velvets as are able to serve many countries, which is the chief merchandise that they send forth. Indeed, they are commonly noted to be great usurers.

One thing I am sure of: that if Ovid were now alive, there be in Genoa that could teach him a dozen points *de arte amandi*. For if Semiramis were ever celebrated amongst the Assyrians, Venus amongst the Greeks, Circe among the Italians, sure there be dames in Genoa that deserve to be celebrated and chronicled for their excellent practice in love. And truly the Genoese themselves deserve that their wives should be praised, because I saw in no place where women have so much liberty. For it is lawful there openly to talk of love with what wife soever she be, insomuch that I have seen young men of reputation, standing in the street, talk of love with young mistresses, being in their windows above, and openly rehearse verses that they had made one to the other. And in the churches, specially at evensong, they make none other prayers. So that he that is not a lover there is meet for none honest company. Many men esteem this as a reproach to the Genoese, but they use it as a policy, thinking that their wives through this liberty of open speech are rid of the rage that maketh other women to travail so much in secret.

Indeed, the women there are exceeding fair and best appareled to my fantasy of all other. For though their uppermost garment be but plain cloth by reason of a law, yet underneath they wear the finest silks that may be had and are so finely hosed and shoed as I never saw the like, open-faced and for the most part bareheaded, with the hair so finely trussed and curled that it passeth rehearsal. So that in mine opinion the supreme court of love is nowhere to be sought out of Genoa.

But like as the women are excellent in this, even so do the men exceed all other in superstition. For there be within the city twenty schools or companies of disciplinants, otherwise called *battuti*, whose manner is when they are called to devotion, as every Good Friday or in the midst of a plague, of famine, of war, or of otherlike occasion that requireth or rogations [3] such processions, they assemble and clothe themselves in sack, linen, or buckram, with their backs naked and their faces covered, saving little holes to look out at. And having certain scourges or whips (some of wire) in their hands, they go about the town whipping themselves that the blood shall run from the back down to the heels, so painfully that it moveth the poor people to compassion. For when this is done, they think God must needs fulfill their prayer. The like whereof is used in all other places of Italy, but because I think no two cities are able to match Genoa in the number of these *battuti*, I thought good to make mention of them here.

Finally, the state is holden by a duke, changeable every two year, who, with eight governors and eight proctors assigned unto him, ruleth the whole for the time. Nevertheless, Andrea Doria, the Emperor's admiral for the middle seas, useth all at his will in matters of peace or war, and almost in every other thing.

The Building of Genoa

OF THE edification of Genoa be divers opinions, but because no certainty is written thereof, I will omit their sayings that ascribe it to Janus, or to Genuus, the son of Saturn, and agreeing with

[3] Rogation as a noun means "request" or "supplication"; here it seems to be a verb meaning "calls for."

the opinion of the Bishop of Nebbio (that particularly wrote the chronicle thereof),[1] I think it to be of such antiquity that neither the time of foundation nor yet the author thereof can well be known. As for the name, it is not unlike but that (because it is the very entry from the seas unto Lombardy) it was first called Janua (a gate or door), and afterwards corruptly Genoa. But how or when it was builded or for what cause it was so named, this is clear: that in the Romans' time, almost 300 years before the coming of Christ, this city ruled the country about it, as appeareth both by a table of brass lately found in the vale of Pocevera [2] and also by the mention that Livy maketh of the destruction of it by Mago, Hannibal's brother, and of the repairing of it again by the Roman consul Lucretius Spurius.

From which time to the coming of Charlemagne into Italy I find nothing notable of Genoa, save that it was one of the first cities that openly professed the Christian faith.

[We omit the medieval chronicles as well as most of the recent conflict and counterconflict with the Emperor and the King of France, in which Andrea Doria bulks large for his victories by sea. Omitting ff. 163v to 186v, we continue with Thomas' discussion of more recent history.]

So that finally, by means of Andrea Doria, the French king's officers were licensed,[3] his galleys by sea put to flight and some taken, and the city restored to her ancient liberty, notwithstanding that many thought Andrea Doria would have taken the rule of it unto himself.

[1] Agostino Giustiniani, Bishop of Nebbio. See the Bibliography.

[2] In 1507, according to Alberti (fol. 20 in 1581 ed.). The plate dated back Genoese existence only to 116 B.C., the destruction by Mago to 209 B.C. Thomas may have seen the plate, which was exhibited in the cathedral; it is now in the Palazzo Municipale.

[3] Dismissed. The year of independence was 1528.

Hereupon a council was called, a new reformation established, a duke, eight governors, and eight proctors chosen according to the order that yet remaineth, and the city ever since continued in peace, with increase of so much wealth and quietness that at this hour she may be reckoned one of the happiest and richest cities of Europe.

And albeit that some stirrings have been since that time for alteration of the state, as the assault that the Conte Guido Rangone made with 10,000 men of the French king's brought out of Lombardy,[4] and the conspiracy that the Conte de Fieschi made now of late [5] (in the which he himself was drowned and Gianettino Doria slain), yet hath the city persevered now these twenty years in one state, much through the great wisdom of Andrea Doria, who (refusing the dominion of it when he might without difficulty have taken it upon him) hath not only restored it to the perfect liberty of a commonwealth but also with his notable service in the Emperor's affairs (as in his voyages to Tunis and Algiers, in the rescue of Coron besieged of the Turks in defense of Barbarossa his armies the years '37 and '38, and in oppressing of the great corsales or pirates by sea) hath so maintained the imperial favor towards the Genoese that no man is able to hurt them at this day. For though, indeed, they be not the Emperor's subjects, yet when any state should happen to move war against them it should well appear that he tendereth them no less than as the dearest subjects he hath. For the which they likewise at all times have and yet do serve him for his money to the uttermost of their powers.

[4] In 1535. [5] In 1547.

The Description of Milan

AMONGST other particular states of Italy, the duchy of Milan hath been one [of] the most notable. For while the house of Visconti reigned, the same valiantly maintained wars of great importance against most puissant princes and powers. And for the interest thereof, the notablest wars of our days have happened between the Emperor and the French king, insomuch that Francis, the first of that name, fighting before Pavia against the imperial army (led by the Marquis of Pescara and the Duke of Bourbon), was taken prisoner and conveyed into Spain; [1] where for his ransom, after a year's imprisonment, he was fain to pledge his two sons and consequently to marry the Emperor's sister, with other covenants too long to rehearse.

And no marvel though these two most mighty princes of Christendom so much contended for this only state. For though in name (being but a duchy) it should not seem great, yet in very deed, both for the wealth of the country and for the quantity, the thing hath been of as great reputation as some realms of Europe. Out of doubt there have been some Dukes of Milan much greater in territory, wealthier in revenues and treasure, more puissant in wars, and, finally, more honorable in peace than divers of them that had kingly titles.

As for the richesse and beauty of the country, I am afeard to speak of, lest to him that never saw it I should seem overlarge in the due praising of it, and lest unto him again that hath practiced there I should seem unwise to treat of that that my knowledge is not able worthily to set forth. Nevertheless, between fear and shame this much will I say: that such another

[1] In 1525.

piece of ground for beautiful cities and towns, for goodly rivers, fields, and pastures, and for plenty of flesh, fowl, freshwater fish, grain, wine, and fruits is not to be found again in all our familiar regions.

I think the Emperor, that now is lord thereof, will confess that he draweth more money yearly to his purse out of that only state than out of some of his realms. And yet his Milanese dominion is not half so much at this present as that that divers Dukes of Milan have had. For whereas the Emperor, besides the city of Milan, hath now seven or eight cities, as Pavia, Lodi, Cremona, Alessandria, Vercelli, Novara, and Como, Dukes of Milan have had some twenty and some thirty cities and upwards; yea, and some so great that they have aspired to the dominion over all Italy, as in the brief history following more plainly appeareth. Nevertheless, he that now shall happen to see the company of noblemen and gentlemen that are in manner continually attendant on the Emperor's lieutenant or deputy in Milan shall say that the same representeth rather the court of some puissant king than the train of a deputy.

And I think verily that Don Ferrante Gonzaga, now lieutenant there,[2] rideth many times more honorably accompanied and with a greater presence of majesty than the Emperor himself doth in Germany.

The like whereof with rather the more is to be said of the Milanese gentlewomen, who in sumptuous apparel may compare with the best, specially in the ornaments of their chariots with coverings of cloth of gold, of velvets, of silks, and a thousand sorts of embroideries. There is almost no craftsman's wife in Milan that hath not her gown of silk and her chain of gold, a thing that should seem rather marvelous than credible. But the craftsmen there are so excellent in their doings and the women so expert in silk works that it is no wonder though their gain grow to the buying of gay gear.

[2] From 1546.

Finally, the city of Milan, standing in the heart of the pleasantest and fairest plain of all Christendom, is served of all delectable and necessary things that are to be desired for man's sustentation, honorable for the court, gallant for gentlemen, harbor for soldiers, delicate for dames, rich for merchants, and wealthy for artificers. But for notable or sumptuous buildings it may not be compared with Venice, Rome, or Florence. For albeit the houses be great and fair within, yet outwardly it is nothing of that beauty and pomp that those other cities be, by reason that for the most part the Milanese building is all of brick, because hard stone and marble is not to be had by a great way off.

Nevertheless, the Duomo of Milan (being their cathedral church) is one of the rarest works of our time, built all of fine marble, so well graven and cut that the workmanship is a wonder. But it is of so unmeasurable greatness that most men doubt whether ever it will be finished or not, though it have many thousand ducats of yearly revenue in good land towards the continuance and a number of workmen daily laboring thereon.

But what speak I of the church? the castle of Milan being so near, which in mine opinion is the worthiest and strongest of all Europe. For it hath ward within ward, fortress divided from fortress, that one may hold against another, walls of endless strength, and large ditches well watered, as fair built overall as needeth to be and so well fortified that without famine it is impregnable. And this, concerning the country, city, and people of Milan, in general shall suffice.

The Beginning and Success of the State of Milan

As LIVY and divers other authors write, the year before the coming of Christ 259, from the edification of Rome 460 and from the beginning of the world 4860, in the time of Ahasuerus otherwise called Cyrus and Longimanus,[1] son of Xerxes and nephew to Darius, Kings of Persia, the city of Milan was rather augmented than newly built by certain Frenchmen called *Senones* or *Insubres*, people of low Brittany now called *Semans*, where likewise is a town called "Milan." These were the Frenchmen that first passed the mountains and settled themselves in Lombardy and that afterwards went under the leading of Brennus to Rome, burned the city, and besieged the Campidoglio, though at last they were discomfited.

[We omit the ancient and medieval chronicle of "the chief market of all Italy" in Roman times and of the city of the Visconti and the Sforza in late medieval times (ff. 189v–198v.]

Thus, Lodovico Moro taken and dead, as is before said, his son Francesco shortly after the Battle of Ravenna,[2] being then but tender of years, was established Duke of Milan by the Emperor's means and continued in the state till the coming of Francis, the French king, into Italy; who with the help of the Venetians chased him away and gat the state of Milan by

[1] Artaxerxes the First, who ruled from 465 to 425; his father, Xerxes the First, is now identified with Ahasuerus. Thomas has interchanged the Christian calendar here with the Roman.

[2] In 1512.

force, leaving Monsieur de Lautrec governor of the same; so that Francesco Sforza withdrew him to Trent and there remained till the Frenchmen, through their tyranny and ill governance, became so hated of the Milanese that at length they were chased away and Francesco revoked home, though in effect he enjoyed it not long. For the French king shortly after with a great power came in his own person into Italy, and so chased Francesco again out of the state of Milan, and prospered much in his wars there until the journey [3] of Pavia, where he with many of his nobles were taken prisoners. After which discomfiture, Francesco Sforza by the Emperor's favor was once again restored to the duchy of Milan and continued in the same till through envy and malice of some pickthanks the Emperor was unjustly persuaded that the said Francesco was not so faithful toward His Majesty as his goodness had merited; so that the Emperor, conceiving an unkindness and a mistrust in him, constrained him by force not only to abandon Milan but also for his safeguard to flee into the castle, which after a very long siege he yielded unto the imperials, to depart freely with bag and baggage.

And so (being letted of the imperials from going to Como where he intended to sojourn till he might clear his innocency towards the Emperor) in manner half desperate he agreed with the Frenchmen and drew to the camp of the league that then was made against the Emperor. Finally, he went into Cremona till, after the taking of Saint Pol,[4] the Frenchmen's doings in Italy went all to wrack. Wherefore, seeing the Emperor Charles the Fifth that now is come to Bologna to be crowned,[5] he went simply thither unto him and there, submitting himself with just excuses, recovered His Majesty's favor, with restitution of the state of Milan upon these conditions following: that the Duke should marry the Emperor's niece, daughter of the King of

[3] Battle (originally a day's fighting).
[4] French general, taken prisoner in 1529.　　　[5] In 1530.

Denmark and of the Emperor's sister; that he should pay the Emperor 900,000 ducats in ten years by equal portions; and finally that, dying without issue, he should leave his estate of inheritance to the Emperor.

Incontinently upon which agreement, Alexander Bentivogli, as Vice-Duke, with divers other officers, were sent to Milan to levy the first payment of this money, which was easily gathered up. For the Milanese, coveting the return of their Duke (whom for his gentle and temperate governance in times past they heartily loved), sticked not to strain themselves for his relief, in such wise that though their customs and taxes were doubled by reason of these payments, yet their hope of better life to come under their Duke made them not to esteem their present charges.

Then came the Emperor's niece,[6] the daughter of Denmark, to Milan, and there was most solemnly received with infinite triumphs and finally married to the Duke in presence of the Cardinal of Mantua, with such feasts and plays afterwards as so great a marriage required.

But ere a year went about, the Duke (through great infirmity blinded of one eye) died without issue,[7] leaving the state of Milan wholly to the Emperor, who ever since hath governed the same by his lieutenants. The first whereof was named Antonio de Leyva, so lame a man of his limbs that he used to be carried on men's shoulders, but on the other side so prudent and ware a captain in his doings as in his days was not lightly to be found again.

Next unto whom followed the Marquis of Vasto,[8] a very honorable and courtly man, but not altogether so happy in his proceedings as such noblemen covet to be.

Finally, after his death, the Emperor hath placed there the famous Don Ferrante Gonzaga, uncle to the Duke of Mantua, whose prosperity hath not only been great in feats of war but

[6] Christina.   [7] In 1535.   [8] Governor, 1538–1546.

117

also wonderful in purchasing of fame through the sincere and rare administration of justice that he useth. I call it not rare for other cause than for the rare correction he hath used against the offenders, whereby he hath won the hearts of them that love justice.

As for the progress of the things happened in the state of Milan since the death of Francesco Sforza (in whom it seemeth the house of Visconti to have taken his end), I shall not need here to make any rehearsal because on the one side the doings of the same have not been very great and on the other side they are present and familiar.

Of the State of Mantua

THE city of itself is very fair and strong and standeth richly, by reason the countries about are plain and no less plentiful than the other parts of Lombardy be. It is strong because the river of Meltio (or Mentio,[1] as some call it), falling out of the lake of Garda through the town of Peschiera, passeth to the Po by Mantua and maketh about it such a pool that three parts of the city are defended with the breadth of a quarter of a mile of water every way, which in some places is deep and in some shallow that it cannot be passed with boats. And then in the necessary places such bulwarks are made to defend that it seemeth impossible to be won by assault on that side.

And for the fourth part, which is toward the west, it is very well fortified with strong walls and bulwarks and a large ditch well watered, besides that the ground on that side is in manner all marsh or at the least so rank that in the driest of the

[1] The Mincio.

summer there can none artillery pass; so that the city is undoubtedly one of the strongest that I have seen.

The dominion that the Duke hath is not great, neither of circuit nor of revenue. For at the best (as I have been informed) the rents never passed an 100,000 ducats a year, and many times it hath been much less, by reason it is not standing but riseth of customs and casualties.[2] It is true that the state is much increased by reason of Montferrato, that the last Duke had by the marriage of his wife; so that now the Duke of Mantua's rents by estimation are reckoned at 130,000 ducats or thereabouts.

And as for notable buildings in Mantua, other than such as be universal in the goodly cities of Italy, I find none, saving certain proper lodgings that the Duke Federico, deceased, hath made on the south part of his palace, which undoubtedly are gallant and rich.[3] Wherefore proceeding now to the original of the citizens and city, with the success thereof hitherwards.

The Original of Mantua

By AGREEMENT of most authors, I find that the people of Mantua are descended of those ancient Tuscans that before the siege of Troy departed out of Lydia in Asia and, under the leading of their prince, Tirreno, came and inhabited the region of Italy. Part of which Tuscans, choosing afterwards the place of Mantua for their habitation, builded the city before the coming of Aeneas into Italy and before the edification of Rome more than 300 years.

[2] Occasional receipts.
[3] Thomas missed the new Palazzo del Tè (1535), which Alberti called *vago et ornatissimo,* "graceful and richly decorated" (fol. 394).

[We omit the origin of the name and then the medieval history of the rulers down to the long line of the Gonzagas (ff. 201–206v).]

And leaving three sons by his wife Beatrice, daughter of Ercole, Duke of Ferrara, that is, to wit, Federico that next succeeded him, Ercole made cardinal, and Don Ferrante that now is the Emperor's general at Milan, finally he [Francesco] died.[1]

After whose death Federico took the estate upon him and was made general of the Roman Church by Bishop Leo the Tenth, confirmed by Adrian the Sixth, and continued also under Clement the Seventh. And as the Emperor (that now is) returned from his coronation at Bologna, passing through Mantua (where he was most honorably received), His Majesty, for the virtue, worthiness, and nobility known in this Federico, called him from the degree of marquis and created him duke.

He married Margarita, daughter and heir of the lord Guglielmo Paleologo, Marquis of Montferrato, in whose right by favor of the Emperor's majesty he obtained her father's estate, that is to say the dominion of Montferrato. And so, notably fortifying the city of Mantua, he died,[2] leaving four sons, Francesco, Guglielmo, Lodovico, and Federico.

Francesco, after his father's death, entered into the dominion, but because he was then of very tender years and passeth not yet the age of fourteen, his father by testament committed the governance of him unto his wife with the help and counsel of his brother Ercole, the cardinal, until the young Duke shall be grown to sufficient years; who, by the parents' consent and by the Emperor's procurement, hath been contracted unto one of King Ferdinando's daughters and shall marry her very shortly, as the saying is.

[1] In 1519.   [2] In 1540.

State of Ferrara

Of the State of Ferrara

FERRARA is one of the notablest cities of Lombardy, as well for
the beauty and greatness as also for the strong site and fortifica-
tion.

First, for beauty, if that part that is called *la terra nuova*
had been thoroughly finished as it was devised, it should have
been worthy for fair streets to have been preferred before
any other city that I have seen. And now as it is, I think it
no less worthy. For you shall find above a dozen streets so
just and evenly set forth that I warrant you there is not so much
as the corner of a house to let a man of his full sight from
the one end to the other. Some of which streets lack little of a
mile long, with the goodly houses and buildings on both sides
so fair and uniform that it seemeth all done at one time and by
one agreement, as no doubt the most part hath been indeed.
And then in the midst it hath a very fair green appointed out
for the market place. But the Duke that now is hath had no
mind to follow it, although his father Alfonso bestowed the
most travail of all his days about it to his wonderful charge, as
he that shall see it may well consider. So that the most habitation of people resteth still in the old part of the city, which is
also indifferent fair but nothing comparable to the new. Then,
as touching the greatness, I think the circuit by the walls be
little less than five miles. And finally, for strength it hath the
goodliest and strongest wall and the largest ditch, well watered,
that I have seen, specially for three parts to the landward. And
as for the fourth part, though the wall be not so strong, yet is it
reputed of no less force on that side than on the other, by reason
that within twenty yards of the wall the great river of Po

121

hath his course down towards the sea, which runneth so swift and is so broad and deep that it is not to be passed of any enemy to give assault to the town.

The Duke hath under his dominion two other cities, that is, to wit, Modena and Reggio, with a good part of the low countries of Romagna, and may dispend yearly by estimation between 200 and 250,000 ducats, and is esteemed very rich because he hath had no war nor other charge of importance for the space of thirteen years or more that he hath governed the state.[1]

The Original and Success of the City

LIKE as of other places be divers opinions, even so is there of the beginning and name of Ferrara. Some will that the name thereof hath grown of a certain quantity of iron that the same city yielded for a tribute unto the lord of Ravenna, as Argenta and Aureolo [1] have also done of the payment of silver and gold. Some other will that it be so called of the mines of iron that have been found there, which opinion is most sensible, considering that *Ferrara* (after the use of the Latin tongue) signifieth none other but the place where iron is digged forth, as Caesar in his *Commentaries,* the eighth book of the French wars, and as Livy in the fourth of the Macedonical Wars, do affirm.

But to pass over these antiquities and come nearer to our purpose, I find that the said city of Ferrara was first closed with walls by one Smeraldo, captain for the Greekish Emperor in

[1] Since 1534. He too had a longer purse than the King of England.
[1] Or Oriolo, near Faenza.

Ravenna, and long time after (being a certain space under the obedience of Henry the Second, Emperor of Almain) it was recovered by the Countess Matilda, daughter of the Conte Bonifacio, as her right inheritance, through help of the Venetians and of the lords of Ravenna, out of the hands of Henry the Third, then Emperor; which Countess at her death,[2] with other her possessions, left it unto the use of the Roman Church, insomuch that long time it was governed of vicars and of legates until the house of Este gat the rule thereof, who first obtained it [3] under condition that they should forever hold it in fee of the Church of Rome.

[We omit the chronicle of the Este rulers (ff. 208v–212) before the sixteenth century.]

[Ercole] leaving his state unto his son Alfonso,[4] who proved so worthy a man that notwithstanding he had married Lucretia,[5] daughter of Alexandro, Bishop of Rome, yet when the same Bishop by force offered to take from him the country of Romagna, he resisted so valiantly that the Bishop was fain to forgo his enterprise. The like whereof he did unto Bishop Leo the Tenth, that purposed to have taken Ferrara from him.

And thus having by Lucretia, his first wife, three sons, Ercole, Hippolito, now cardinal, and Don Francesco, and by Laura, his second wife, two sons, Alfonso and Alfonsino, he died.[6] After whose death, Ercole, as eldest son, entered into the estate and at this day enjoyeth the same.

And albeit that hitherto there hath happened no notable occasion to try his worthiness, yet can he not choose but prove well. For he is a goodly man of personage, high of stature, strong and well proportionate in all his members, bald on the crown of the head, and amiable enough of countenance. He

[2] In 1115.   [3] In 1195.   [4] In 1505.   [5] Borgia.
[6] In 1534.

hath a good wit and is somewhat learned, and indifferent in the administration of justice. And one thing special I remember of him worthy to be recited. The Emperor at his being in Italy borrowed money of all hands. And demanding amongst the rest 100,000 crowns in loan of this Duke, he brought him a bag of 50,000 crowns, excusing himself that to lend 100,000 crowns he was not able, but to give His Majesty those 50,000 he could be contented with all his heart, and by this shift kept the other 50,000 crowns in his purse.

Finally, of religion he is no more earnest than most princes are, and in his life he followeth the court of love, to lose no time of pleasure.

He is friendly to fair women and cherisheth change. By his father's days he married Madame Renée, daughter unto Lewis the XII, French king, a very gracious lady, by whom he hath two sons, Alfonso and Luigi. Hitherto he hath maintained his dominion in peace and is therefore thought (as I have said) to be very rich. He is well furnished of artillery and munition and of devotion is altogether French, so that if there should happen any business in Italy between the Emperor and French king his part is like to be therein.

The State of Piacenza and Parma

PIACENZA and Parma are two notable cities of Lombardy, lying between the Apennine Hills and the river of Po, whose territory and pastures are so fat and sweet that it is thought no place of all Europe able to compare with it for the excellent cheeses it maketh, which by the name of Parmesans are right well known over all.

These two cities of late appertained unto the Church of Rome, but Paul the Third, now Bishop of the same, a Roman of nation of the house of Farnese, to increase his own family found the mean to separate these two cities with their territories from the Church's dominion and to give it unto his own son, named Pietro Aluigi,[1] creating him Duke thereof, and in recompense annexed unto the Church the duchy of Camerino that he had before taken by force from the Duke of Urbino.

This Pietro Aluigi, being the year of our Lord 1546, entered into the estate, began to bear himself over stoutly against the nobility of the same and specially toward the Signor Jeronimo Pallavicino di Cortemaggiore, who, rather disdaining than envying this man's dominion, was fain at last to flee and to abandon wife and children, goods and lands. Insomuch that this new Duke took all unto himself and furnished the castle of Cortemaggiore (being a very stronghold) with his own men, took all the rents (being 12,000 ducats a year) to his own purse— except a small portion assigned to the lady wife of Jeronimo for her living, with condition, nevertheless, that if she relieved her husband with any part thereof, she should lose the whole. Besides this, he oppressed his subjects, causing them to buy harness and to furnish themselves for the war on their own cost. But most of all, he occupied a great number of laborers in his works, beginning the foundation of a strong castle in the place where the Abbey of St. Bennett's in Piacenza stood. The monks whereof he appointed unto a spital house called St. Lazarus in Campagna. And these laborers were taken up by force from all parts of the Parmesane and Placentine, of which there perished at one time, with the fall of an hollow bank, above fifty persons; so that what with one thing and what with another (being also a man known full of abomination in all kind of vices, and specially in the unnatural), in conclusion he became hated of all men, insomuch that the Conte Giovanni

[1] The notorious Pierluigi.

Anguissola and the Conte Agostino di Pallavicini, with certain of their kin and friends, conspired against him, and at their time appointed, finding him with a small guard in his own house in Piacenza, slew him, hanging afterwards the dead body out at a window for a spectacle unto the people.

Finally, these gentlemen (foreseeing the danger that for this doing might follow unto them in case the state should continue of the Church) practiced before with Don Ferrante Gonzaga to see whether he would back them by receiving the strong city of Piacenza unto the Emperor's behoof; so that, being at a point with him, the matter was so handled that the next night after the Duke's death there were secretly received into the town eight hundred of the Emperor's men and so the city won without stroke-striking.

All the money, plate, jewels, and stuff that could be found of the Duke's, to the value of 30,000 crowns and upwards, were divided amongst the confederates and the Conte Giovanni Anguissola, who killed the Duke with his own hands, allowed by the Emperor twenty men for his guard.

Finally, the Bishop of Rome (being hereof advertised) incontinently caused Parma to be fortified and furnished with men of war and tempted by corruption of money to have had one of the gates of Piacenza delivered him by night; but his practice was discovered and certain Spaniards therefore taken and hanged. And ever since, for more than this half year, the Emperor's power upon the Placentine and the Bishop's on the Parmesane have kept diligent watch and ward, looking every hour for open war. What it will prove to, He best knoweth that governeth all.[2]

---

[2] Pierluigi's son Ottavio, though he was the Emperor's son-in-law, did not obtain full possession of the duchy until 1556.

Of the State of Urbino

THE city of Urbino standeth almost on the top of the Apennine Hills, in manner between the Mark of Ancona and Tuscany, the people whereof (as Pliny writeth) have been surnamed *Metaurensi,* and it seemeth to have taken name of *Urbes Binae,* two towns. For who that well considereth the proportion of it shall judge by the miter fashion thereof that it hath been two towns joined together, and the middle, which is a hollow descent between two hills, is the slenderest part of the city.

The Duke's palace is a very fair house, but not so excellent as the Conte Baldassare[1] in his *Courtesan* doth commend it.

The Duke's dominion is two cities, Urbino and Pesaro; his revenue passeth not 60,000 crowns by the year. But his ancestors for the most part served other states, as the Duke that now is also doth, whereby they kept much greater ports than their own ability would bear.

Amongst other, this Duke's father builded an house within a mile of Pesaro, called *Imperiale,* which in mine opinion is one of the best devised little things that may lightly be found. It standeth on the side of an hill and hath prospect both to the city and to all the valley; it hath many fine little chambers, goodly open vaults, and excellent fair fountains. But that which most of all pleased mine eye was that, being of a great height, you may out of the highest garden ride about on the top of the house, which is very fair paved with brick and railed on both sides with fine pillars and rails of white marble.

As for the edification of Urbino, or other notable memory

---

[1] Castiglione. Hoby's English translation, published in 1561, was entitled *The Courtier,* using the established English word.

before the year 1345, I find nothing new to be written. At which time (by reason of the variance between Bishop Clement of Rome and the Emperor Lewis of Bavaria, who to make their parties strong made divers new lords in Italy) Galasso di Montefeltro was made vicar for the Emperor in the cities of Urbino and Eugenio [2] against the Bishop of Rome and his adherents; in which his succession continued inheritors unto the year 1444, that Frederick, after made Duke, obtained the estate. The occasion whereof was that Guido, Conte di Urbino, having no heir male by his first wife, feigned that he had gotten a concubine with child, and so secretly took the son of his near kinsman Bernardino della Carda, which even then was newly born, and, naming it Frederick, caused it to be nourished as his own.

Not long after his wife died and, marrying again, [he] engendered a son named Oddo, who indeed succeeded the father in his estate. But he was so vicious of living and so busy with gentlemen's wives that in a sudden rumor of the people he was slain, and a protonotary called Carpesiano with him.

Whereupon this Frederick, the putative son, by the whole voice of the people was elected their prince; [3] who in his youth had been very well brought up, specially in feats of arms, in the exercise whereof he lost one of his eyes.

This Frederick was not only valiant but also very well learned

[2] It was a later Montefeltro, Noldo, who was made imperial vicar by the Emperor Louis the Fourth; Noldo was lord of Urbino, and the Eugenio seems to be an error.

[3] Ruling from 1444 to 1482. Federigo, who is well known from the Piero della Francesca portrait with the broken-nose profile, is now thought to have been the illegitimate son of Guidantonio (not Guido). Bernardino Ubaldini della Carda was Guidantonio's son-in-law and a Florentine exile; hence perhaps the legend that made Federigo his son and part Florentine. See Filippo Ugolini, *Storia dei Conti e Duchi d'Urbino* (Florence, 1859), pp. 213–215.

and so happy a man that in his time he was general of eight several armies and died captain of the Venetians' army in the field before Ferrara.

The Bishop of Rome for his worthiness made him Duke; the King of England not only gave him money but also made him of the Garter, for which courtesy all Englishmen have a certain privilege of freedom in his dominion; and the French king made him also of his order. Besides that, there was none state in Italy but that at one time or other presented him with some worthy gift.

And above all the rest, his fidelity seemeth to me most worthy of commendation. For when Francesco Sforza was forsaken of all his other friends and pursued with 20,000 men, he only received him and thereby put himself and his whole state in jeopardy, which he determined rather to lose than to seem an unfaithful friend, and, in effect, maintained Sforza till time served him to recover.

After the death of Frederick, his son Guidobaldo, of the age of twelve years, succeeded, who reigned quietly about twenty-one years till the coming of Valentino Borgia, son of Alexander the Sixth, Bishop of Rome; that first by such craft gat the state into his hands that Guidobaldo was fain to flee disguised in a plowman's clothing. Nevertheless, through the good will of his subjects he recovered his state in short time again. But Valentino's force was such that at length the Duke took such treasure as he had and fled to the Marquis of Mantua, whose sister he had married, and there, dying without issue,[4] ended the house of Montefeltro that had reigned in Urbino the space of 157 years.

Valentino Borgia held it but a very small space, for shortly after his father's death, Julius the Second, Bishop of Rome, persecuted him and brought the house of Borgia to naughts,

[4] In 1508.

and thereupon gave the state of Urbino to his nephew, Francesco Maria Prefettino della Rovere, whom he created Duke there.[5]

This Francesco Maria was a very wise and valiant prince —nothing inferior to Frederick before named—who reigned not fully ten years, but Leo the Tenth that succeeded Julius the Second made a puissant army and expulsed him out of his state and razed the walls of the city even to the earth. Whereupon he established his nephew, Juliano de' Medici, Duke in his place, and after his death (for he lived but a while) his brother Laurence de' Medici; who continued in the same till Adrian the Sixth that succeeded Leo expulsed him and restored the state unto Francesco Maria, that enjoyed it till he died,[6] the space of sixteen years, in so great reputation that all princes and states of Italy loved and honored him, and the greatest of them were glad to entertain him for their general in the wars, wherein he gat infinite sums of money. But he was so great a builder and so liberal unto his soldiers that when he died he left no kind of money in his coffers.

By his lifetime he builded the palace beside Pesaro called *Imperiale* and fortified the city of Pesaro and the castle there with divers other goodly buildings, and gat Katherine, daughter and heir to the Duke of Camerino, to be married unto his son Guidobaldo, that now liveth; in whose right he enjoyed that estate during the father's life.

As soon as Francesco Maria was dead, Paul the Third, now Bishop of Rome, seeing this Duke that now liveth a young man without money or great friends, made so great a power against him that for fear to lose the whole he was content for a little money and some other small recompenses to yield to the Bishop

---

[5] In 1508. *Prefettino* was a nickname, meaning "the little prefect," his father being prefect of Rome.
[6] In 1538.

the state of Camerino, which the Bishop hitherto enjoyeth. And yet for all this, the same Bishop hath found the means to marry his niece to the same Duke; whereat many men marvel not a little.

Finally, this Duke Guidobaldo is general over all the Venetians' lands, towns, and fortresses and hath of them 10,000 crowns' annuity. But hitherto he hath had none occasion of trial in the wars. He is mean of stature, hard of favor, and very grave in countenance. And though he be well learned, his wisdom hath had no great trial as yet, but men trust he will prove as virtuous as his predecessors.

The Conclusion

THERE be divers other states in Italy, specially the commonwealths of Siena and Lucca, the bishopric of Trento, called *Tridentum* in Latin, Piombino, Mirandola, Castel Geffroie,[1] and suchlike, but because they are not of such reputation, either for dominion, power, or continuance of years, that they should be numbered amongst the principal, I have forborne to speak particularly of them, though some indeed deserve notable praise, beseeching all gentle readers to accept my travail and diligence used in this behalf as a thing done for their commodities. And though I want learning and eloquence to accomplish so high an enterprise as to describe pithily the states of countries and commonwealths, yet since I spared no pain nor labor to do profit, I would at the leastwise for my reward crave good report.

[1] Castel Goffredo, south of Brescia.

Imprinted at London
in Fleetstreet in the house of
Thomas Berthelet
Cum privilegio ad imprimendum solum
Anno MDXLIX

Bibliography and Index

Bibliography

The Works of William Thomas

The historie of Italie, a boke excedyng profitable to be redde: Because it intreateth of the astate of many and diuers common weales, how thei haue ben, & now be gouerned. London: Thomas Berthelet, 1549. 445 pp. (STC 24018)

(Second edition.) *The Historye of Italye.* . . . London: Thomas Marshe, 1561. Identical pagination. (STC 24019)

[The *DNB* article on Thomas cites a third edition of 1562, "with cuts," but no such edition is now known.]

Principal Rvles of the Italian Grammer, with a Dictionarie for the better vnderstandyng of Boccace, Petrarcha, and Dante: gathered into this tongue by William Thomas. London: Thomas Berthelet, 1550. Two parts: 68 pp. and 292 pp. (The *Dictionarie* lists some 9,000 words.) (STC 24020)

(Second edition.) (The same title, adding:) *Newly corrected and imprinted.* London: Thomas Powell, 1562. Identical pagination. (STC 24021)

(Third edition.) (The same title, adding:) *in the yeare of our Lord God, 1567.* London: Henry Wykes, 1567. (STC 24022)

Il Pellegrino Inglese ne 'l quale si difende l'innocente, & la Sincera vita del pio, & Religioso Re d'Inghilterra Henrico ottauo, bugiardamente calōniato da Clemēte vii & da gl' altri adulatori de la Sedia Antichristiana. (No author, no translator, and no place of publication named, but dated at the end 1552.) 144 pp.

Bibliography

The original English is in five manuscripts, of which the apparent earliest is in

(1) Cotton Vespasian D.XVIII, a collection, partly autograph, of William Thomas' writings, many of them for Edward VI, but the "Perygrinie," as it is here entitled, is by a professional copyist (ff. 46v–81, or 70 pp.). Errors and omissions make it less accurate than

(2) Additional 33,383, entitled "Pelegrine" (ff. 1–65r, or 129 pp.), a fair copy. Closest to the preferred (2) is

(3) Bodley 53, in a collection of mid-sixteenth-century Protestant tracts (ff. 71–102, or 64 pp.), entitled "Pelegryne." Latest and least accurate is

(4) Harley 353, a later (ca. 1600?) collection of fair copies of state papers, etc., where (ff. 8–36, 58 pp.) is "A Relacōn of a conference had betweene Williame Thomas Clarke of the Councell to Kinge E. vjth & certaine Italian gentlemen in his trauailes: touchinge the Actions of Kinge H. viij intituled Pelegrine. an. 1546."

(5) A copy of (3) is Lambeth Palace Library MS 464 (142 pp.).

The Cotton version (1) was edited by Abraham D'Aubant in *The Works of William Thomas* (London: J. Almon, 1774). The Harley version (4) was edited by J. A. Froude as *The Pilgrim* (London: Parker, Son, & Bourn, 1861).

The Vanitee of This World. London: Thomas Berthelet, 1549. 72 pp. (STC 24023)

[This sermon on eschewing the pleasures of this world in order to follow Christ is entered in the *Short-Title Catalogue* under William Thomas. It is dedicated to Lady Anne Herbert of Wilton, whose father may have been a patron; but nothing in the content relates the work in any way to the William Thomas we know.]

Thomas left two other works in manuscript:

A translation into English of Sacrobosco (John Holywood), *De Sphaera*: MS Egerton 837. [This work of the thirteenth century, which was still in use as a textbook, had been printed since 1472 (Ferrara), and it is possible that Thomas translated from a copy printed in Italy.]

Bibliography

A translation into English of Josaphat Barbaro, ". . . Two voiages that I made thone vnto Tana [Crimea] and thother into Persia": MS Royal 17.C.x (126 fols.). This work was edited by Lord Stanley of Alderley in *Travels to Tana and Persia* (The Hakluyt Society, XLIX [1873], 1–101).
[The account of these journeys, made by a Venetian nobleman from 1436 to 1451 and from 1474 to 1478, had been published in *Viaggi fatti da Vinetia, alla Tana, in Persia, in India* . . . (Venice, 1543, ff. 3–64; 2nd ed., 1545). It was followed in the *Viaggi* by an account of the embassy of Ambrosio Contarini to Persia in 1474 to 1477, which Thomas also translated, and which was printed in the Hakluyt Society volume. Both Italian narratives were reprinted by Ramusio in his great collection of *Navigationi et viaggi*, vol. II (Venice, 1559).]

Thomas' political essays in Cotton Vespasian D.XVIII were included in *The Works*, ed. Abraham D'Aubant, as "Disquisitions on Affairs of State"; only "Pelegrine" (above) was printed with them in this volume.

The most accurate study of the life of William Thomas is by E. R. Adair, "William Thomas: A Forgotten Clerk of the Privy Council," in *Tudor Studies* (London, 1924), pp. 133–160.

Authors Quoted by Thomas

ANCIENT:

Cassiodorus Senator (ca. 490–585 A.D.). *Institutiones divinarum et humanarum litterarum* (extracts published 1528).
Frontinus (ca. 40–103 A.D.). *De aquis urbis Romae* (1486).
Josephus (37-ca. 95 A.D.) *Of the Jewish War* (Latin translation of the Greek original, 1480).
[The single reference to Josephus concerning the arch of Titus suggests that Thomas did not need to consult the work itself.]
Livy (Titus Livius, 59 B.C.–17 A.D.). *Ab urbe condita libri* [*142*] (1469).

Bibliography

Pliny the Elder (ca. 23–79 A.D.). *Historia naturalis* (1469).

Strabo (b. 63 B.C.). "Geography" (Greek edition, 1516; Latin, 1471).

Suetonius Tranquillus (fl. 98–138 A.D.). *De vitae XII Caesarum* (1470).

Varro (116–127 B.C.) *De lingua Latina* (1471 [?]). [The etymologies in book V include those of Roman place names —hills, markets, gates, etc.]

Vitruvius (fl. temp. Augustus). *De architectura* (1486).

Flavius Vopiscus (fl. 300 A.D.). [*Vitae XII Caesarum*] (edition with Suetonius by Erasmus, 1518).

MODERN:

Flavio Biondo, or Flavius Blondus (1388–1463). *Roma instaurata* (written 1446; published 1481).

——. *Italia illustrata* (written 1453; published 1474).

Pandolfo Collenuccio (1444–1505). *Compendio delle historie del regno di Napoli* (1543).

Bernardino Corio (1459–1519?). *Patria historia* [of Milan, in Italian] (1503).

Andrea Fulvio (fl. 1510–1543). *Antiquitates urbis* (1527; Italian edition, 1545).

Agostino Giustiniani, Bishop of Nebbio (1479–1536). *Annali . . . della . . . republica di Genoa* (1537).

Niccolò Machiavelli (1469–1527). *Historie fiorentine* [to 1492] (1532).

Bartolommeo Sacchi, called Platina (1421–1481). *Liber de vita Christi ac omnium pontificum* (1474).

Marco Antonio Coccio, called Sabellico (1436–1506). *Rerum Venetarum ab urbe condita decades IV* (1487).

Raffaele Maffei (Volaterranus) (1455–1522). *Commentariorum urbanorum . . . . libri* [38] (1506).

Bibliography

Some Authors Consulted for the Notes

Leandro Alberti. *Descrittione di tutta Italia.* Bologna, 1550.

Mariano Armellini. *Le Chiese de Roma dal secolo IV al XIX.* 2nd ed., 2 vols. Rome, 1942.

Horatio F. Brown. "The Constitution of the Venetian Republic and the State Archives," in *Studies in Venetian History.* London, 1907. I, 293–334.

Gasparo Contarini. *De magistratibus & republica Venetorum.* Paris, 1543.

Étienne du Pérac. *I vestigi dell' antichità di Roma.* Rome, 1575.

——. *La pianta di Roma.* Rome, 1577. Ed. F. Ehrle. Rome, 1908.

Hermann Egger, ed. *Römische veduten.* 2 vols. Vienna and Leipzig, 1911–1931.

Rodolfo Lanciani. *Ancient Rome in the Light of Recent Discoveries.* Boston, 1888.

——. *Pagan and Christian Rome.* Boston, 1893.

——. *The Ruins and Excavations of Ancient Rome.* Boston, 1897.

Giuseppe Lugli. *I monumenti antichi di Roma e suburbio.* 3 vols. Rome, 1930–1938.

Giovanni Bartolommeo Marliani. *Urbis Romae topographia.* Basle, 1538(?).

Lucio Mauro. *Le antichità della citta di Roma.* Venice, 1542.

Sebastian Münster. *Cosmographiae universalis libri VI.* Basle, 1550.

Franciscus Schott. *Itinerarii Italiae rerumque Romanarum libri tres.* Antwerp, 1600.

Filippo Ugolini. *Storia dei Conti e Duchi d'Urbino.* Florence, 1859.

INDEX

141

Index

Dellabarba, Bernardino, 61
Della Rovere, Francesco Maria, 59, 130
Della Rovere family, 130-131
Donato, Francesco, Duke of Venice, 87
Doria, Andrea, 61, 87, 106-107, 109, 110, 111

Edward VI, King of England, x
Elizabeth, Queen of England, xiv
Emperor: rule over Naples and Milan, 16-18, 90, 113; elected by princes of Germany, 20; *see also* Charles V *and* Maximilian I
Emperor of the East, 20
Emperor of the Turks, 20
Este family, 123-124
Evelyn, John, xviii

Farnese, Alessandro, *see* Paul III
Farnese, Ottavio, 62, 126 n.
Farnese, Pierluigi, 62, 125, 126
Farnese Palace, 53
Ferdinand V of Spain, 57, 58, 91, 92
Ferrara, x, xxi; description of, 121; dominion and revenue, 122; extent of, 18; history, 122-124
Florence, x, xvii, xxi, xxvi; dominions and revenues, 97; manners, 96, 97, 105
— description, 93-97: site, 93; bridges and talisman, 93-94; spring flood of Arno, 94; splendor of buildings, 94-95; citadel, 95; Villa di Castello, 95-96
— history, 60, 94, 98-105: warred against by Pope and Emperor, 60, 94; founding, 98; success of Lorenzo de' Medici, 99; surrender to France, 99; restoration and re-expulsion of Medici, 100; subjugation by Pope and Emperor (1530), 100-101; rule of Alessandro de' Medici, 101-102; rule of Cosimo, 103-105
Francis I, King of France, 60, 61, 112, 115, 116

Franck, Sebastian, *Weltbuch*, xviii, xix
Frederick, King of Naples, 91
Fulvio, Andrea, 23-25, 45-46

Genoa, x, xix, xxvi, 17; dominion and revenue, 107; flagellants, 109; foreign trade, 107-108; government, 109, 111; women, 108
— description, 105-109: site, 105-106; harbor, buildings, Riviera, 106; Doria palace, 106-107; lighthouse, aqueduct, 107
— history, 109-111: origin, 109-110; independence from France, 110; wealth and safety under imperial favor, 111; failure of invasion and revolution, 111
Giovio, Paolo (Jovius), *Commentaries of the Turk*, xiv
Gonzaga, Ferrante, Lieutenant General of Milan, 113, 117-118, 126
Gonzaga family, 120
Gregory V, Pope, 20
Grimani, Antonio, Duke of Venice, 86
Gritti, Andrea, 85, 86

Hadrian, Emperor, 31-32, 52-53
Handford, John, xvii
Harding, George, xvii
Harvel, Edmund, x
Henri II of France, 61
Henry VIII, King of England, xiv, xv, xvi, xvii
Hoby, Thomas, x n., xvi, xvii, xxvii
Homer, xvi, xxiv

Inquisition, xv-xvi
Italian language, x, xi, xii-xv
Italian literature, x, xi, xii, xiii, xiv, xv
Italy: appeal to foreigners, 10, 11, 12; "civility," xvii-xviii, 4; educational advantages of, 10-11; government of, 19; husbandmen, 14-15; justice, 19; law of inheritance, 11; merchant

142

Index

Swiss mercenaries, used against France, 59
Sylvester, Pope, 55-56

Thomas, William: life, ix-xi; his *History of Italy*, ix, xi, xvi, xvii, xxiii-xxvii; his *Italian Grammar*, x, xi, xvii; travels in Italy, x, xi; impressions of Italy, xxiv-xxvii; his *Pelegrine*, xxvii; emotions at the sight of Rome, 21
Toledo, Don Diego de, Vicerè of Naples, 92, 104
Trent, bishopric, 131
Tuscany, xix, xxvi, 18; *see also* Florence

Urbino, x, 18; description, 127, 130; history, 128-131

Valla, Lorenzo, xiii, 56
Vasto, Alfonso, Marquis of, Governor of Milan, 117
Venice, x, xvi, xviii-xix, xxi, xxv, xxvi; Jewish usurers, 69; loans, 81; provinces and cities, 18, 68; revenues, 68-69
— description, 63-68, 86: site, 63-65; ship entrances at Malamocco and Lido, 65; buildings, 65-67, 86; wells, 67-68
— government and laws, 69-78: Doge, 69-70; *Capi*, 70; ducal counselors, 71; *Signoria*, 71; the Ten, 71; the Senate, 71; law officers, 71-72; health officer, 72; Great Council, 72-73; method of balloting, 73-74; civil servants, 74; local governors (*Podestà*), 74, 77; lords treasurers and treas-ures of St. Mark's, 75-76; courts, 76-77; *sindaci*, 77; law's delays, 78
— history of, 57, 58, 61, 84-87: in league against Charles VIII, 57; despoiled by Julius II, 58, 84; in league against Louis XII, 58, 85; in league against Turks, 61, 86-87; naval battle of single ship, 61, 87; defeat by French at Brescia and Ravenna, 85; in league with France, 86; loss of Nauplia and Malvagia, 86
— living customs, 80-83: reputation as misers, 80-82; lewdness, 82; freedom for strangers, 83; freedom of religion, 83
— military organization, 78-79: foreign generals, 78; ship captains, 78; marriage with the sea, 78; temporary dictators (*provveditore*), 78-79; license to carry weapons, 79
— provision of charity, 79-80: provision of grain, 79; charitable societies, 79; hospitals and orphan asylums, 79; *Lazaretto*, 79-80; semiannual delivery from debtors' prison, 79
Vitelli, Alexander, 104
Vopiscus, Flavius, 23

Wilson, Thomas, xvi
Wyatt, Sir Thomas (the elder), xiii, xiv; *Certain Psalms* (1549), xii
Wyatt, Sir Thomas (the younger), xi

Zizimo, brother of the Sultan, 57